Happy 50th Sally
to a great cook
and our
"Queen for a day"

Laurie

(with loads of help
from Charles!)

What's Cookin'

Jack Bailey.

WHAT'S COOKIN'

BY JACK BAILEY

Illustrated with photographs

CLEVELAND AND NEW YORK

THE WORLD PUBLISHING COMPANY

Published by THE WORLD PUBLISHING COMPANY
2231 West 110th Street · Cleveland 2 · Ohio

CW

*Most of the photographs in this
book were made by* FLOYD HOPKINS

*All rights reserved
Copyright 1949 by The World Publishing Company
Manufactured in the United States of America*

To Carol

THE BELLE OF THE MUSSELSHELL

(*a swell dish herself*)

PREFACE

It seems that in every publication there must be a preface. Some big star or some big name always writes it for the alleged writer. As I get it, a preface is something thrown in the book to make it sell, so being more interested in that than anyone I know, I have taken care of my own preface—turn, if you will, to the next page....

THE AUTHOR

CONTENTS

PREFACE

1.	A List	15
2.	Laden Ladles Make Laden Tables	21
3.	Fish	53
4.	Stolen Recipe Section!	55
5.	The Potato Patch	75
6.	Easy on the Tummy	91
7.	Egg Edibilities	97
8.	Bailey's Best	109
9.	Quickies!	127
10.	Canapés, Canopys, Hors D'Oeuvres	139
11.	Vegetables	149
12.	Saludas to Salads (Si)	159
13.	Desserts	173
	INDEX	183

ILLUSTRATIONS

Jack Bailey.	frontispiece
Some things to keep the cupboard from bare.	14
Now we eat.	20
I don't like to fish.	52
I admit stealing every blame dishful in this section.	54
Good "spuds" is good.	74
He has to have a special dish!	90
Where did that come from?	96
These honeys have become a personal triumph.	108
The dropper-inners.	126
No canapé at Waikiki!	138
Don't be fooled—there are no carrot recipes here.	148
A head of lettuce.	158
The cake has fallen!	172
When you come to the end of a perfect meal…	181

What's Cookin'

Some things to keep the cupboard from bare.

CHAPTER ONE

A LIST

> *Some things to keep the cupboard from bare.*
> *Some things we find most generally ain't there.*
> *Things we'd have if we'd stop to think—*
> *And without most of them,*
> *All our meals will . . . not be so good.*

I have often wondered why someone didn't make a list of things to always have on hand in the house, cupboard, icebox, garage, pantry, cellar, attic, back end of the car, or just *anyplace* on the premises so that when you want them you've got them. Now in sitting and wondering, I wondered so long that I wondered why I didn't make the list, or at least start it and then leave enough space for you and myself to add to the list of what the grocery calls staples. Now why don't we just call this evergrowing list

WHAT EVERY STAPLE HAVER SHOULD KNOW
(Use your own head and your own pencil)

Everyone will think first of salt and pepper, so we'll leave that out.

Salt and Pepper
Sugar
Tea
Coffee
Paprika
Onions

Canned Vegetables
Canned Potatoes
Canned Fruits
Canned Meats
Canned Milk
Canned Rattlesnake
   (I'm kidding)

I have a hunch you have all this stuff and many other items of their ilk, so why don't I try to muster up some things I'm always without, and I'll bet a lot of you folks are too, so here's a list of, shall we say, *un*staple staples.

Boxes or cans of prepared bread crumbs
Tomato paste
Anchovy paste and jars
Pitted ripe olives
Soy sauce
Celery and garlic salt
Tuna, salmon, shrimp, and crab
Mushrooms
Can opener
Water chestnuts
Bottle of Maggi Seasoning
Maggi's Bouillon
Beef Bouillon
Prepared chicken fat

Prepared seasoned bread crumb dressing
Cans of sardines
Lots of evaporated milk
All kinds of soups
Oh, yes; Dog and Cat Food
All condiments
Garlic and wine vinegar
Cooking sherry
Vitamins
Fritos, parched corn, and such
Can opener
Boxed cookies
Sharp knives

A List

All herbs
Chili—Tamales
Cocktail frankfurters
Noodles, spaghetti, macaroni
Prepared waffle, biscuit, and pancake mix
Prepared cake and pie mix
Jellos, gelatin
Clams
Can opener
Cheeses and cheese spreads
Crackers and Roundies
Prepared popcorn and peanuts
Mints and candies
Dainty paper napkins
Variety of pickles
Frozen foods
Can opener
Dressings for salads
All types of consommé
Cook books
Zwieback and pre-toasted breads
White and brown rice
Potted chicken and turkey
Wax paper
Can opener
Fresh walnuts, pecans —nuts
Wife or husband

NOTE TO THE EDITOR, PUBLISHER, COOK, HOUSEWIFE, AUTHOR, READER, CRITIC, RICHMAN, POORMAN, GARBAGEMAN, CHEF:

The following empty pages are for us and our list, so here we go for a chronicle of culinary contents that, silly as they sound, will make you a bit of a hit in your kitchen. Fill in your empty list and then turn to page 21. That'll be Chapter Two!!!

A List

Now we eat.

CHAPTER TWO

LADEN LADLES MAKE LADEN TABLES

I expect that since before flint and steel fires or rubbing two sticks of wood together to make a fire, other people have been telling other people how to cook a meal. Now the forthcoming group of stovish stars are not the run of the mill. *You* can roast, bake, broil, fry, sear, sauté, boil, steam, barbecue, ... er ... er ... well cook. That isn't the idea of this book. All your own dishes you can make—soooooo, inasmuch as I'm running out of paper (and you know all those things anyway), we'll just jot down a few tricks of entrees and main dishes that might be a shade different. Okay? Okay!!!

A Chicken in a Port

Most people I know like chicken—and usually get it the same old way. So most people that like chicken will like this new switch on good old chicken. Here's what to do:

Buy or steal 2 frying chickens weighing about 2 pounds each, and cut 'em up into serving pieces. (Toss out or keep for soup the necks, backs, and tips of wings.) Do not brown but melt about ½ cup of butter in a casserole and when hot, add the chicken pieces and cover it up right away. Have the fire low and simmer for at least ½ hour. Whip on a little salt and pepper and add 1 cup of white port wine. Cook this for another ½ hour and slurp in ¼ pound of whole canned mushrooms. Cook this about 15 minutes more, then stir in 1 cup of cream sauce mixed with 1½ cups of cream. Cover again and simmer for another 15 minutes or until the chicken is tender. Now, when this is ready to serve, sneak in ½ cup of sherry and reheat in a slow oven. Now to top the whole thing after you have fixed it the way it is above, sprinkle a thick covering of warm, chopped browned almonds over the top and serve it from the casserole. Toss up a green salad, pull some bread apart, de-top a can of vegetables, and watch 'em go for this Chickie deal.

Pippin' Pot Roast

A usual pot roast is a bunch of stuff tossed into a pot with a roast. This is almost the same with the exception of a few added stuffings into the roast that's surrounded by the pot. See what you think:

Laden Ladles Make Laden Tables

Get a 4- or 5-pound pot roast and lard it (or have the butcher) with strips of salt pork, making the incisions run with the grain of the meat. Put it in your favorite Dutch oven and brown it in bacon fat. Now it's browned, add ½ cup of chopped celery, a dozen tiny onions (or slice a couple of big ones), ½ cup of diced carrots and 1 teaspoon of minced parsley, a bay leaf, salt and pepper. Dump in a can of consommé and 2 cups of white cooking wine. Put a hood on the dish and slowly and reverently cook on the top of the stove for about 4 hours. That's all—except you thicken the wonderful gravy, cut, and serve. Now we've done that—we eat.

A Stuffed Leg (Pork)

A leg of pork is a leg of pork, even if it's only a leg of pork . . . *but* . . . you can make a creation by just this little change:

Have your butcher bone a leg for you. Take it home and fill it with your favorite dressing (I use the same as in turkey or chicken). Sew up its leg or clamp it with skewers, and roast it in a hot oven for about ½ hour, then turn to medium and cook according to weight. About 40 minutes per pound. cooks—do me and the folks a favor. Don't put water or anything in the roaster. Just roast your leg with the fat side down and salt and pepper on top. You'll have leavin's for gravy, tender pork, and a real swell smash of a success by doing it this way. (*Editor's note:* He's right.)

Shades of Lamb Shanks

Sure and you'll be happily surprised at this shading of shanks. Cooked this way, many people will be thinking they're something else. Give them your thanks, *but they're still lamb shanks.* First, get out your pencil and figure out how many you're going to feed. One shank per serving. Got it? Then let's go:

Important: Don't let butcher crack the bone. Now, salt and pepper each one and roll same in flour. Take some fat and melt it in a roasting pan, slap in the shanks, and brown in a pretty hot oven. After they're browned, add some sliced onions and a mere squiggin' of garlic. Season again with celery salt, sage, poultry seasoning, and coarse black pepper. Now sprinkle a little water lightly over the whole thing. Put lid on and bake in a medium oven for 1 or 1½ hours. Thicken the gravy and make up a pretty looking plate, decorated with whatever you can find. Speaking of finds, this shank thing is a *real* find.

Beef Stroganbailey

A round of round steak, a little patience, a little spice, and seasoning will make this a delicacy. Look—listen—but don't stop. Carry on:

Cut 1½ pounds of round steak in strips about 2 inches long and ¼ inch wide. (You know to cut it cross grain, lest it gets tough.) Put some butter or bacon fat in a skillet, heat, and add beef strips. Cover and cook for 15 minutes. Stir it now and then. Between stirs cut in small pieces ½ pound of mushrooms. Add to meat and cook another 10 minutes. Might need a bit more butter. (If no fresh mushrooms use 1 small can of chopped mushrooms.) Now put meat and mushrooms in top of a double boiler. In same skillet melt 1 tablespoon of butter, add 1 tablespoon of flour, and stir till blended. Continue stirring while adding 1 cup of sour cream. Bring to a boil, pour this over the meat and mushrooms in the double boiler, and cook over boiling water for 15 minutes, with an occasional stir. Season with salt and pepper and serve. Serve with rice browned in olive oil, which you'll find listed in the rice department. If I forget the rice department, brown rice in olive oil, then boil in water and chicken fat until done.

Chops of Lamb en Vino

Lamb chops are usually either broiled or fried. What say we take a new slant and casserole the little fellas. Won't take long to catch the idea. It's like this:

Grab your earthenware casserole and brown about 6 large *loin* chops. Do this in butter with some small whole white onions and a few young tender carrots. Naturally you season with salt and pepper and pinch in a few mixed herbs. To zoom it up a bit, slip in ½ cup of dry white wine and, if you want, about ½ pound of mushrooms (sliced) won't hurt. Cap casserole, cook, slow, for 30 minutes—and that's it.

Chops of Pork en Loaf

Chop-chop on this one, and mighty fittin' too. The pork chops and dressing combo you are about to know about is about as nice a dish as you can know about. Now let's know about it:

Forget about the pork chops for the moment and let's make some dressing first. Simmer ¼ cup each of finely chopped celery and onions in a couple of tablespoons of butter, don't brown just simmerize. Now pour over this 2 cups of bread crumbs and mix all lightly. Add ½ tea-

Laden Ladles Make Laden Tables

spoon of sage, 1 teaspoon of salt, and ½ teaspoon of pepper. Now add 2 tablespoons of chopped parsley. Now, the pork chops. Where were they? Find 'em? Good. Place a pork chop in the end of a baking pan and smear some of the dressing between chop number one and the one you are about to put in. Keep chopping and dressing away until the pan is full. Don't spare the dressing. Bake this in a slow oven for about an hour and a half. Might have a spare chop to close off the top layer and it will seep through and keep the whole loaf sort of sealed up. This when finished and served will stop all talk of hunger for this meal. Yipe.

Lamb Leg Luscious

The good old leg of lamb is always good, but a sauce and a trick might make it a shade "gooder," so if you have a leg of lamb on hand and a few spare moments, try this. If you haven't a leg of lamb on hand, but the few spare moments, go get a leg of lamby and do this:

Rub it thoroughly with garlic, and rub it good. Now cut loose with a couple of tablespoons of butter or some bacon fat in a roasting pan and brown our little leg on top the stove. Add a chopped onion, a bay leaf, sprinkling of thyme, a few sprigs of parsley, and 2 cans of consommé. Put on a lid (on the roaster) and simmer either on top of the stove or in a slow oven for about 3 hours. Leave the lid on all the time—don't monkey with it. Now in the 3 hours you'll surely have time to brown 2 tablespoons of butter in a stew pan, then add slowly 2 heaping tablespoons of flour and brown again. Slip in a can of consommé and stir until it's smoothly and thickly. When the 3 hours are up and the lamb is cooked, add the strained juice from the pan and cook together 5 minutes. Push in 1 tablespoon Worcestershire and taste for seasoning. Stir in 2 cups of chopped green olives and cook until well heated. Carve the lamb and pour the sauce over the lamb and serve. I'm sure everyone knows about removing the skin to keep the strong taste away and also, there's a duct to be removed. I don't know what or where it is, but the good old butcher always does. Don't forget it. As I said above, I will repeat again, "The good old leg of lamb is always good."

Steako Pineapplo

Now this one you have to make up as you go along like I did. With a little trouble and lots of luck this steak will come out with a taste you'll be glad for. Easy too:

Marinate in a glass dish some T-bone steaks. One per person. Marinate in a dash of olive oil, salt and pepper, pinch of cayenne, several slices of pineapple and about half the juice of a small pineapple can. Cook as you like—

Laden Ladles Make Laden Tables

broil, fry, or bake. Do not marinate over an hour, and, let me add, the flavor will make people talk for longer than the marination time. Simple, and while it coasts in the marination period you can prepare the rest of the dinner. (Takes about an hour to open the vegetable cans if your can opener is as dull as ours.)

Navy Beans Lambie

Usually, to make the ordinary beans, a ham hock is used, or a bit of used pork, or a strip or two of salt pork. Now I have in "Bailey's Best" a bean recipe, but to show you the other side of beaning, take a try at this beanery and you'll find a pert and tasty beanish thing worth while:

Take the remainder of a leg of lamb you have used the day or so before. The bone and whatever clings to it is the base. Cook it with navy beans, a bit of garlic, a can of solid pack tomatoes, some onions, a carrot or two diced fine, a stalk of celery minced, a little chopped parsley, salt and pepper, and let the whole bunch of stuff simmer for 2 or 3 hours. When no one is looking add a little red wine (just a nip). If this sounds good and you haven't any left over leg of——, get yourself a few lamb shanks, roast them in the oven, n' then start the whole procedure as above. They're not the usual beans but they are beans that will surprise you as even me. . . .

Smooth, Slick, Souffléed Beefola

Here's a cutie. A conglomeration of good stuff put together with careful hands, watched with careful eyes, but carefulness stops when eaters eat it. That's good, and so is beefola. Do it thusly:

You start the soufflé with a sauté, a sauté of ½ pound of ground beef, ½ pound of ground fresh pork in a tablespoon of cooking oil. Well-cook the meat and then add 1 teaspoon of salt, 2 tablespoons minced parsley, 2 tablespoons finely minced green onions, and stir in 1 cup of thick cream sauce. Now beat the yolks of three eggs and stir in. Beat the egg whites by their little selves until they stand in peaks. Fold in (peaks and all) the mixture and then grease yourself a baking dish, set in a pan of hot water, and bake this in a moderate oven for about 45 or 50 minutes, or until the thing is firm to the touch. Take it out, serve with it whatever sounds good with it, and watch above-mentioned eaters have at it.

Roast Pork Chinatown

I am very fond of Chinese food, lots of people are. Never have I ceased to rave about Chinese-style roast pork, along with other folks. I went to trouble to find out about it, but it's no trouble to make:

Laden Ladles Make Laden Tables 31

In a mixing bowl make up a batch consisting of 4 teaspoons of sugar, 1 teaspoon of salt, 1 teaspoon of honey, 3 teaspoons of soy sauce, and 3 tablespoons of chicken bouillon. Stir, stir, and stir again. Now cut about 2 pounds of fresh pork butt or shoulder of pork lengthwise in 3 pieces. Soak the cut pork in above batch for about an hour, turning it now and then. Remove the good old pork from the batch and place on a rack in a roasting pan, adding a bit of water to keep it from smoking. Roast in a moderate oven for about an hour and a half. Turn occasionally. Serve sliced with English mustard.

Plainish Pot Roast

People pleasantly partake of pot roast permanently. Here's the way the Bailey does it, so read it, try it or forget it. We like it often, maybe you will. Hope so. Here goes:

First, look up a pot with a tight lid or you're out of luck. Good luck. . . . Now take 3 or 4 pounds of top round beef and sift a little sifted flour over it. Press and massage the flour into the meat. Put some suet or beef drippings in the pot and heat until she sizzles. When sizzling put in meat and brown on all sides. When you are browning the last side, add 2 or 3 small onions and sprinkle meat with salt and *black* pepper, add a cup of *boiling* water, and 2 teaspoons of A-1 or Worcestershire, whichever you like best. Now slap the lid on and let it simmer for 2 hours. If water cooks away, add more *boiling* water. About a half hour before it's done, add a #2 can of tomatoes if you want to. You don't have to, but it has been done. Nothing tricky—but plenty slick and edible. May have some soon myself.

Ham That Am

Brothers and sisters, here is ham like you always hoped ham would be: It is—make a note of this following deal —a real meal:

Get a center cut of ham about 2 inches thick, put it in a pan and cover it with water—boil it for 2 minutes and drain the water. Now place dear old drained ham in a baking dish and spread the top with prepared mustard (not too thick), sprinkle brown sugar all over it, and kind of blend with mustard. Now pour in just enough milk to cover it. Wait until your oven gets to moderate temperature and then put this in and bake for about 40 minutes. Hey—during baking time lift ham once in a while so milk will get under it. If milk bakes away add more and don't worry when it curdles, it always does when being baked. Now remove ham to hot serving platter and sift a little flour in pan, add ¾ cup of milk, place over open flame and simmer for about 3 or 4 minutes, stir it constantly, and then strain this gravy over

Laden Ladles Make Laden Tables 33

the ham. Need I say serve this with yams or sweet potatoes, a lot of corn bread or biscuits, and you'll be singing the praises of the ham that really am. Yes, mam.

Chipped Beef Creamed

This is the same old lovable chipped beef creamed, but do this little stunt first—pull the beef apart into small pieces, then in a wire strainer, run cold water over it for a second or two. Drain it, stir it into the cream sauce and simmer, stir and serve. (Excuse me, but I like it over melba toast—ever try it that way?)

Slumgullion

Horrible name, but honey of a dish. Good for ya, cooks a long time with little trouble which allows time for you to do things that are good for you too, like reading the paper or listening to the radio. All right here we go, but not on the radio:

On the stove place a large stewing pot about ⅔ full of water. In same, place about 3 pounds of stewing beef cut in hunks. Salt and pepper this and boil for about an hour and a half. Then add a cup of diced celery, 2 medium onions sliced, a cup of carrots, and a heaping handful of celery leaves, more salt and pepper, some garlic salt, a dash of Lea and Perrins, a dash of beefsteak sauce, a handful of rice, a handful and a half of macaroni. Cook and stir, stir and cook until the meat is really tender. Watch it a bit as it has been known to boil dry or stick to the bottom, so watch and stir, stir and watch, and in case of emergency add more boiling water. Be sure you have a tight-fitting lid on this pot at all times unless you're adding water or cooking and stirring. This is as good if not better the next day. It's better also if not too thin. The gooier the gooder most folks think. I do, too.

Macaroni Gratoni

This is a double-header dish. Dinner or supper one night, next day the remainder makes a fine salad base. If you are worrying about getting fat you'd best skip this whole thing, but if not carry on in this manner:

Into a large pot of water boiling like the dickens, dump 1 package of elbow macaroni and let 'er go for about 10 minutes. Drain and in a well-greased baking dish place a layer of macaroni and a layer of grated American cheese, keep this up until the dish is full or you're out of stuff. Over this pour about 2 cups of thin cream sauce and then cover with bread crumbs. Bake in moderate oven for about 30 minutes and bread crumbs are browned. So much for the main dish of an evening. The next day, with the remainder that by now should be cold, cut up some

Laden Ladles Make Laden Tables 35

sweet pickles, add about a teaspoon of ground parsley, a mixture (thick) of cream and mayonnaise, and drop of tabasco. Mix all together lightly and you will have some kind of a salad. So much for the double-header, eh?

Curry for Cooking Capers

Lots of leftovers are just plain left over, and too often *thrown* over the back fence. Tsk. Tsk. Make the following curry mixture and for so many leftovers it will remain a fixture. Make like so:

Peel and cut up a small apple, add 2 tablespoons of chopped onion and put into a frying pan with 2 tablespoons or more of butter. Let this brown and smash into a paste, then add 2 teaspoons of curry powder, a pinch of powdered clove, and 1 teaspoon of lemon juice. Now simmer this slowly for 10 minutes (until well blended). The mixture is now ready for you, and vice versa. Now cook some rice with plenty of water. Take some of the rice water (little) and put in the curry, then the gravy left over from the meat. Now place the leftover cooked meat in this gravy and cook for 10 more minutes. Always serve curry with rice and the following curryable leftovers: chicken, beef, veal, lamb, pork, sausage, or anything else you think curryable. Fittin' food for fightin' budgets.

American-Style Guylas
(Hungarian Goulash, then)

In less than hour you can take your folks to the table with a dish that's keen. Yep:

Just get yourself 2 pounds of lean veal, cut it up in small pieces, and roll in flour, pressing as much into the meat as you can with your fingers. Put a pot on the fire with some beef drippin's or other fat, and when it is sizzling hot, drop in the veal and add 1 tablespoon of salt and 1 tablespoon of paprika. Stir this around until thoroughly brown and mixed, then add 1 cup of hot water, 1 small onion cut up fine, and a small kernel of garlic. Cover the pot with a lid and cook very slowly until meat is real tender. The gravy will thicken and brown in cooking, and the flavor will be wonderful. Ought to have a cabbage handy on this day, either cooked or for salad. They go hand in hand with goulash. This dish will go hand in hand with your menus.

Laden Ladles Make Laden Tables 37

Big Baked Veal Cutlet or Ghiveci Cu Carne

I like that last name better and I think it means the same thing as the first four words—but whether or no, this recipe in your files will mean a smash hit on your dinner table. This beauty is for four but heaven help you if they're hungry (or do you do as I do and wait until everyone is so hungry anything tastes good). Here, now, is the way of the big baked cutlet:

To have a big one you must get a big one, so get a 2½-pound veal cutlet. After you talk the butcher into it and prove you're not balmy, take it home, get set for a bout with said veal. Melt in a baking dish about 3 tablespoons of butter or beef drippin's. Salt and pepper cutlet and put it in the baking dish. Over it pour a large can of tomatoes, add a little bud of garlic sliced fine, and smear in good with the tomatoes. Now add ½ can of tomato soup and 1 cup of water. Turn on your trusty oven moderate and bake for an hour. While that is going on, slice some string beans diagonally, thin, and boil for about 10 minutes (if you are lazy as me, use a can of string beans, but the others are better). Dice a couple of medium onions and fry them in a little butter until golden. Then push the onions to one side of the skillet and in the cleared part put 2 tablespoons of flour, keeping the frying pan half over the medium flame but only under the flour. Keep stirring flour until it is good and brown, then add the other ½ cup of tomato soup and a cup of cold water. Mix all of this thoroughly and bring to a boiling point, then add the string beans and let all boil for about 3 or 4 minutes. Now as your mouth waters, add this last concoction to the veal that cooked low this hour and bake this whole thing for 20 or 30 minutes. Now when you have done as cited above, cooks, you've done something. It sounds so good on paper you can almost smell it. Not the recipe, I hope, but the results. Ah, I'm getting hungry—may have this for dinner tonight, why don't you?

Chicken Carolyn

Carolyn is my wife's full name and has nothing to do with the chicken, but I thought I'd better name a recipe after her because she has so many relatives, will be flattered and write them all, thus I can sell more books. What a market if this works.

You start in the usual manner by buying 2 nice fresh fryers (I still think the secret of good chicken is getting real fresh ones). Have the butcher cut them in serving pieces, then put pieces in a large paper bag that has flour, salt, and pepper. Shake the bag real good and the washed damp chickens will get an even coating of the flour and seasoning. Now in several good skillets put a lot of *fresh* Crisco. Be sure and use fresh as other fats change the

Laden Ladles Make Laden Tables 39

taste. When the Crisco is really sizzling hot, brown the pieces of chicken to a light golden brown. While you're doing this have the oven at moderate temperature, but leave the door open. As each piece is ready, put in the baking pan—I always place each type together, dark meat at one end, white in the center, etc., for it makes it much easier to serve and fill requests at the table. After all the browned chicken is in the pan, take the grease mostly out of one skillet and pour in enough water to cover the bottom of the baking pan and about two inches deep, salt and pepper water, and bring to a boil —do not add flour. Pour this over the browned chicken and put a lid on right away. Let this steam for at least 1½ hours. About ½ hour before serving remove lid and the chicken will turn out nice and brown, crisp enough yet not dried out. I have had much success with this method and the raves and requests "to do it again" are a good guarantee. I use a regular roaster and make cream gravy in it after the chicken is removed to a hot serving platter. Shall we say, "A plattery for flattery."

Loafer's Meat Loaf

Here's meat loaf that is good when you are tired of cooking but getting hungry along with others you must serve. Probably isn't the most unique recipe in the world, but it's easy and good and doesn't take long to whip up.

Get 1 pound of good ground sirloin or round, ½ pound of fresh country sausage, and blend them together well in a mixing bowl, or if you're going to cook it on top the stove, use the same pot (one with a tight-fitting cover). After meat is blended, break an egg in it and knead with hands. Now a little salt and quite a bit of pepper, a shot of tabasco and Worcestershire. In the palm of your hand crumble some *fresh* soda crackers, and knead the whole thing again, then form in loaf if to bake, or smooth it out if pot on stove. Pour over this a good quantity of sweet catsup, and then instead of having onions all through it, I always ring several sweet onions and place over the top on and in the catsup. That's all, bake the regular way, or if on top, cover and steam. The onions will flavor the meat either way, but when served, "them" that don't like onion too much can scrape them off. Success to us Lazy Loafers.

Legless Pork Roast

This is so simple I was afraid to try it at first . . . but being simpler than usual, I did. Don't be scared, kids, just do it. Then laugh at other folks who putter, fume, and fuss over roast leg of pork.

For 4 or 5 servings, get about 4 pounds of good roasting pork. Take a pot with a tight-fitting lid, wash the pork, salt and pepper, place in hot pot, fat side down, nothing else. Cover it tightly and go sit down. Get up once in a while and turn it. When nice and brown and done, get up again and serve it. Then sit down again and eat it.

Patty Sausage Grits en Circle

Being a man from the deep south (of Iowa) I am very fond of hominy grits. There must be two or three thousand ways of cooking these gritty little grits, but a mess that's become one of my favorites was given me by an old schoolteacher. She taught better than she cooked or I wouldn't be so ignorant, but on occasions she cooked better than she taught. Like this hominy, sausage, patty in a circle for instance. Might go after one of these dishes sometime when you are fresh out of ideas. (You can use other things besides sausage, like—oh, well, any kind of a patty you think would be good.) But here's the original, according to her.

Take some regular old-fashioned bulk sausage and season it up a bit with some finely chopped chives. Now boil some hominy grits and cool them in a flat pan. When cool, cut them with a cookie cutter in little round circles. Next roll the little circles in flour. Now take your chived sausages and mold them into the same size as your hominy grit circles and roll them in flour. In separate pans fry each section of this section until brown. Place the patty of sausage on the patty of hominy grits and serve it right up. You can put parsley around the patty circles, or fresh onions, radishes, or carrot sticks.

You know how to make crisp carrot sticks? Listen. Take fresh carrots, slice lengthwise in about ¼-inch strips, put in a fruit jar full of water, and then in the icebox for a couple hours. When you take them out after this they are really good and crisp. Mighty good with so many things, better try it.

Chop Suey Home Choice

A number of kitchen cut-ups would love to show off and make a Chinese dinner, but get scared out at the very thought of it. Now don't be scared at all, you don't even have to be brave—just be careful and take a little time. Run the recipe through, and do like I say. Don't look at the title and say phooey—go ahead and make this Chop Suey. In a Dutch oven put a little fresh fat and 1½ pounds of lean pork cut in about 2- to 3-inch strips. Cover and steam *but do not brown*. Be sure pork is done, but remember, don't brown it. When pork is cooked add 2 large sweet onions, quartered and sliced thin, then at the same time add 1 small green pepper, deseeded, cleaned, quartered, and sliced. Cover this again and cook till tender. When above has happened add 1 tablespoon of Chinese brown sauce (looks like molasses), 1 tablespoon

Laden Ladles Make Laden Tables 43

of soy sauce, 5 cups of fresh celery in 2- to 3-inch strips, cutting celery lengthwise in about ¼-inch strips and above length. Now add 5 cups of washed fresh bean sprouts (if you use canned sprouts add later). Now recover this and cook until *not quite tender*. Don't get it mushy—that happens to chop suey too often. Now take a small quantity of cornstarch and mix with cold water. Don't add too much as it will get too thick and ruin what you have done so far. Now add a small can of button mushrooms and about ½ cup of ½-inch-square green pepper, 1 small can of water chestnuts split and drained, and ¼ cup of small strips of canned pimento. Simmer this about 5 minutes and add 1 large fresh tomato cut in eighths. Cook a minute or so and eat. While above is cooking, roast some almonds, cook 1½ cups of rice (or my fried rice recipe someplace in this book). To serve, on each plate put a handful of heated canned noodles, pour mixture over it, the tomato on top, rice on side, and almonds over mixture. For vegetable cook 1 cup China peas in pod, adding salt and ¼ tablespoon sugar.

Appraised Braised Ribs

For both praising and good eatin' make up an oven full of this. You have the meat, vegetables, and potatoes, which leaves you 2 hours for bridge, poker, making the salad, and taking a short hike. Maybe even you can read the evening paper or listen to the radio. That's up to you, but the recipe is up to me to write down, then it's back up to you again to do it. Now do it. The reason I mention the two hours of leisure is account when I first ate this Appraised Braised I thought you had to stand over it and nurse it along. Not true, so allow the time and allow me to get on with the concoction. Concoct thusly:

Melt some nice bacon fat, about 3 tablespoons of it, make serving hunks out of 4 or 5 pounds of short ribs of beef, and sear in the hot fat until good and brown on all sides. Add some sliced onions, a smashed clove of garlic, salt and pepper. Now here's where you pinch just a pinch of mixed herbs, then dissolve 1 bouillon cube in 1 cup of warm water and pour over the whole thing. Lid the pan and roast in a slow oven for the 2 hours I've mentioned. Between hikes, reading or what-not, baste it as often as you think of it. Oh, wait a minute, you got to get up at the end of the first hour and peel about 6 potatoes and 6 fresh carrots. Then run back and sit down after you add them to the meat that's cooking. Now at the end of this hour (thus adding up to 2) remove the meat to a hot serving platter, make some nice thin gravy, call the folks, and go to it. I don't know how you feel, but ribs have the sweetest and most wonderful taste when slowly cooked like this. Be sure the meat is real done-ish, or leave it in the oven a little longer if not. Now I'll quit on the Appraised Braised as we may get into the third hour.

Laden Ladles Make Laden Tables 45

Noodleburger Casserole

Hamburger—cheeseburger—nutburger, all kinds of burgers. But friends, a noodleburger in this manner and baked in a casserole is a full-fledged filling feed, and a meal in itself. You try—you see. Here now is the way to go about this. Finely chop ¼ medium-sized onion and brown it in some bacon drippings. When nice and brownish mix in a pound of ground round or ground sirloin and continue with the cooking business until the ground meat is brown. With your favorite stirring spoon start stirring a while. First stir in a can of cream of tomato soup and 1 cup of water. Now mix and stir in 2 cups of *uncooked* noodles and continue cooking until the noodles are tender—watch this a shade and stir in more water if necessary. Season with salt and pepper to taste and add 1 can of creamed corn. Now butter your casserole and pour this stuff in it. Cover with at least a cup of grated cheese only, and bake in a medium oven for at least 45 minutes. Six souls can be made happy on the Noodleburger, and with dishes like this all coming out together (maybe with a baked potato for each eater) ((a bit of salad)) (((some good coffee))) ((((dessert)))) as I was saying or about to say, the cook will enjoy the meal too, and live longer. This is one of my very favorite recipes.

Chork Pop Pie or Pork Pie with Chops

As the fancy cookbooks say, this is an En Casserole, but that shouldn't scare anyone out. As a matter of fact, you can do this in any baking dish, but the point is it's good, savory, sure-fire. As usual a lot depends on the butcher man. If you get the wrong cuts (as so often happens if you aren't in good with him) the whole thing should be called off. Now here's what to do:

First smile, show your teeth (if any), and ask the dear, dear butcher to cut you some thick but lean pork chops. Thank him, pay him, and hurry home. The minute you arrive home boil some potatoes in jacket. When they are on, any time you feel like it slice and chop and hack up a green onion (top and bottom). Put some grease in a skillet, salt and pepper the precious chops, throw in the onion, and sauté all for about 6 minutes on each side of the chops, tossing onions over on each turn. Now put this in a buttered casserole or buttered baking dish and add about ½ teaspoon of dry mustard and a little shaved ginger root (if you have it). Pour a cup of sour cream (either prepared or fix some yourself) over this whole bunch of stuff. Then peel and slice your boiled spudatoes and arrange on top of this whole thing. Salt and pepper and then bake in a medium oven for at least 30 minutes. Somehow this comes out so much better than you think that you will be mighty thankful for me thinking of putting it in the book. Nothing trick, but something that tastes soooo good. I'll bet the price of one of these books you'll get requests to repeat this recipe, and you'll be glad to do it, 'cause you'll like it too.

A Sausage Cabbage Head

So many of our friends are afraid of cabbage, its results and odors. Now forget that and again refer to the section on vegetables and check on that cabbage cooking deal. It has always worked and the forthcoming Sausage Cabbage Head is worth a whirl. Wow, what a flavor—like an old Germanic specialty. Get ahold of some good rye bread, a very light salad (or even macaroni-type salad) and then proceed in the fashion to follow:

I think a pound of good fresh link sausages would be the first thing. Now whilest you are shredding ½ small cabbage, drain a can of tiny new potatoes. Okay. Brown the sausages in a skillet, and when brown remove them to one side and brown the canned potatoes in the same skillet, then butter a baking dish and place potatoes on the bottom. Sprinkle some parsley on this and then place the grated cabbage on top of this. Remember the browned sausages? Go find them and then place them on top of the cabbage. Take a can of chicken consommé, strain it, and pour over the whole batch. Bake for about ½ hour (covered) in a medium oven. This will handle about four but well.

P.S. Just remembered something. Y'needn't bother pre-cooking the cabbage. Put it in the deal raw. The steaming that automatically happens serves the principle of non-odor and non-aftereffect.

Author

Riced Liver

Here is a light and little dish to prepare and it takes a whale of a recipe to beat it. So maybe it cooks a little long, but think of the things you can be doing while it's cooking. Seems like this silly thing is usually a hit, because the blending and steaming give it a swell natural flavor. It's not only good to eat, it's pretty to look at, too.

Take down your trusty skillet and brown about a cup of raw rice. Not too brown, but brown it good. Put it in a buttered baking dish or casserole. Now sauté about a pound of beef liver in 2-inch squares with a couple of minced onions. Add this to the browned rice and pour over the whole thing 3 heaping cups of beef bouillon, with a little thyme and some salt and pepper. And now, my friends, all you have to do for 45 minutes is cover this and let it simmer. Then add some frozen

Laden Ladles Make Laden Tables 49

lima beans (teenie weenies) and cook for 15 minutes more. Now whip up a bit of toast, some hot coffee, and some fresh fruit and cheese for dessert. What more could you want for a bit of a different dinner. Look— no potatoes. The whole dinner is there except for a light salad, the coffee, and the dessert. Good luck to you and and your liver. Yum, yum.

Buckeroo Potluck

I know an old desert hombre, name of Floyd Hagen, Sr., who sits under a cactus plant most of the time in the Lucerne Desert. Yep. But when "supper" time draws nigh, this old gent gets up off the sand and if he's in the mood whips up this wonderful combination. If he ain't in the mood he opens a can of beans. Now I'm frank to admit this tastes better out on the desert, or at least in the open, but it's mighty good inside eatin' too. So here's to the Buckeroo.

Pardner, draw yourself a trusty Dutch oven with a lid. Now haul off and peel and thickly slice some white spuds. When you've skinned the spuds, heat about 4 tablespoons of bacon grease in the skillet, then quarter about 3 Spanish onions and brown them lightly, then put in the spuds and be sure it's in a layer over the onions. Sprinkle over this a diced clove of garlic. Now cut up a batch of bacon in 2-inch strips and lay over the whole thing, then quarter another Spanish onion (medium one) and put over the top. Now pour in some hot water, enough to come up about two-thirds of the skillet. Cover and simmer until the potatoes are cooked but not mushy. Of course, every time you think of it, slap in a little salt and pepper. Now, here's something good if you're prospectin' around for something a shade different, but the eater's gotta be rugged and hungry. Tear off some hunks of sourdough bread, wilt some lettuce, and eat this, and then call the doctor if you eat too much. If there's any left and the doctor gets there, give him some too, because by the time he gets there you'll be all right and he'll be hungry, so fill him up and send him back to the office. Hit the trail on this one, hombres, and you'll find it smells as sweet as a new saddle.

Stuffed Veal Chops with Stuffin'

Supposin' ya got about five people coming in for dinner and you want a little something that isn't too tough to make, but something that seems a little different. You will personally like this dish and your guests will be shouting about it. There isn't really much trouble to get this thing cooked up, and the flavor and the idea will get a bunch of raised eyebrows.

So we've got five coming in, let's get 5 veal chops, but thick. Say an inch and a half thick. Now make up some

Laden Ladles Make Laden Tables

good old-fashioned and well-seasoned bread stuffin'. On each chop now, make a deep gash (on the outer side). Fill each gash fully with the bread stuffin' and fasten down with toothpicks. Now coat the chops with seasoned flour and dip each one in a beaten egg batter, then re-dip in fine crumbs or meal. Fry these little fellers until they are brown, and then cover the pan and let cook slowly until done. That oughta take about a half hour or so. Sauté some apple rings, put a bit of cinnamon on top of apple rings, and serve. What goes good with this is some real, real, real, real thin sliced raw potatoes browned in fresh cooking grease. Toss a salad and put on some cranberry sauce and there's a real fine and dandy meal for anyone. As a matter of fact, for *every*one. If you have more than five coming in, get a chop a head. Go ahead.

I don't like to fish.

CHAPTER THREE

FISH

> Fish
>
> *I don't like to fish, and I don't like fish.*
> *If you like to fish . . . fish.*
> *If you like fish . . .*
> *Use your own recipes or steal the neighbors.*
>   *Forgive me.*

I admit stealing every blame dishful in this section.

CHAPTER FOUR

STOLEN RECIPE SECTION!

So many people swipe ideas and recipes and then lead you to believe that a wonderful dish is a little something they dreamed up one day over a hot stove and an empty pot. I hate jails (and the food is terrible), so I am going to come clean and admit stealing every blame dishful in this section. What's more, to keep my nose clean and shy away from lawsuits I shall reveal the name of the victim. But you be fair too. If these "copped" culinary concoctions don't turn out so well, write *them*—not me.

Dunstedter's Dandy (Pot Roast This Is)

Purchase yourself a round bone roast (pretty good size if your family is pretty good size). Pierce the meat in two places and stuff in a clove of garlic in each pierce. Salt it and pepper, using ground pepper. Cut a lemon in two and squeeze it all over the meat. Brush the whole hunk of meat with your favorite steak sauce, but don't brush it so hard you get all the lemon juice off. Sprinkle with dry mustard and kind of make this into a thin paste.

Pick it up slowly, as by now she's pretty slippery, and put in a Dutch oven. Brown slowly in suet. Add some onions and cook until they're yellow. Add a little boiling water, but don't pour over the roast, just get it in the Dutch oven and not too much. Add a medium can of mushrooms and cover. Let her rip along, not too fast, for about 2 hours.

Just about the time you figure you're getting a good deal on the pot roast, make this mustard sauce for it. (This sauce is keen on a lot of other things, but you figure out what.) A half teaspoon of ground pepper, ½ teaspoon of Coleman's mustard, 1½ tablespoons of Heinz' 51 sauce, ½ teaspoon of Lea & Perrins, and a fair-sized chunk of butter. Put this in a pan, and as it cooks add fresh cream or as close as you can come to it until it looks and smells about right to you. *Don't let this sauce boil.* Pull out the meat, put on the sauce, then stand up and take bows for your overwhelming success as a chef.

NOTE: *The victim of this stolen recipe is the famous Eddie Dunstedter—band leader, arranger, composer. But perhaps his biggest claim to fame is his organ playing. You've heard many of his symphonies and enjoyed them, and now, may you enjoy this next "Symphony in Sauce."*

Dunstedtersspareribsandsauce

Before we get into the sauce department, here's a cute caper about the preparation of the ribs before barbecuing. Parboil the ribs *slightly* to remove some of the fat, and then the cussed things won't be so apt to burn on the grill. Pretty slick, eh?

Here we go on the B.B.Q. Sauce, ready or not. A couple of onions chopped fine. (Let your wife or a guest do this.) One bottle of Heinz catsup and one bottle of Heinz chili sauce. A half cup of Coleman's mustard and a good slug of A-1 Sauce, same type slug of Lea and Perrins. A double jigger of soy sauce and a handful of salt and pepper. Hope your hand isn't too big. A few dashes of tabasco (easy, girls, on this), and a little vinegar. Stir this until it's thoroughly mixed. Now paint ribs and barbecue. Paint before and during barbecue. A good idea is to make more than you need because this sauce is really fine on a lot of stuff you cook inside.

Geller's Goulash

When you got a bunch coming in for a sort of sit around and eat off your lap deal, this is a hodgepodge that will handle their case and not run you nutty with fussing over it. You got plenty of other stuff to do, with hors d'oeuvres, little gags to munch on, etc. There will be a section on that stuff too, so check it later. Right now, look at this. (I ate this at Geller's once and it was right good. Incidentally, he stole it from a Doc Richards in Janesville, Ohio. Right now, Jack Geller runs the Geller Theatre Workshop in Hollywood, one of the finest theatre schools in the country.)

Slice a whole bunch of potatoes. Dice a whole bunch of white or Bermuda onions and have on hand a whole bunch of ground round steak. Now take a good-sized baking pan or dish. Start making layers of the above with salt, pepper, and a sprinkling of butter. Keep putting in additional layers of this in the order named until you have enough to cope with the oncoming appetites. When the pan is as full as you think you'll need, pour a *large* can of tomatoes over the top and then add quite a little more butter on top. Bake this in a slow oven (350°) for 3 hours. Keep your little blue eyes on it, and if it starts getting away from you turn the oven down. Put one of those pear and cheese salad deals on the same plate, or peach and cottage cheese combination, and you're all set with hardly any trouble in preparation. You see, this dish helps you be the maitre d' and still allows you to be the life of your party if you want. And who doesn't?

Stolen Recipe Section! 59

Spaghetti with Meat Sauce

I've always been scared to try spaghetti until Betty Furness, beautiful and talented actress, invited me over to her house one night. I promptly confiscated the recipe and will slip it to you at once. Best I ever et:

In your favorite saucepan put 2 tablespoons of olive oil, 2 tablespoons butter, 1 chopped onion, and a clove of garlic chopped fine. Heat, melt and stir this a short time, then dump in ½ pound of chopped raw pork and ½ pound of chopped raw beef. Dice ¼ pound of mushrooms and add to above. Let this merry little group simmer along for about 10 minutes. Now here we go: Add the following: 10 shakes of Maggi (don't shake Maggi too hard), 2 teaspoons soy sauce, 1 small can of tomato paste, 1 tablespoon chopped parsley, 3 cups of brown sauce.

Note to reader: Details of brown sauce herewith. Five tablespoons flour, 5 tablespoons butter, 3 cups of stock (½ teaspoon "BV" to one cup of water), salt and pepper to season. Brown flour and butter together, turn off heat, and add stock and bring to a boil. Add 2 tablespoons chili sauce and 2 tablespoons sherry if desired. As I said, add the brown sauce, salt and pepper the whole batch of stuff, and pinch rosemary. Excuse me—add a pinch of R. Cook this slowly for at least an hour.

Boil spaghetti in salted water (1 teaspoon salt to 1

quart) for 15 minutes. Drain. Pour hot water over. Pour sauce over the steaming hot spaghet—get her out on that table hot, mam, and serve Parmesan cheese on the side.

Season Shrimp Creole

I'm sure most everyone has "in-laws." I've several, and one of the best any guy could have is a gal in Miami Beach, Florida. She's my wife's sister and her husband is a big shot down there—but in spite of all this she's a good cook, too. I swiped the socks off this recipe so I have to salute my sister-in-law, Mrs. Claude Renshaw.

Boil a goodly batch of shrimp for about 10 minutes. But add this to the water and believe you me it makes the makin's. Add a generous flavoring of vinegar and all your favorite spices. This is one of those dishes you keep sniffing until it savorizes. Be sure it's tarragon and add some oreganum—*and* a clove of garlic. Now, clean in the usual way and marinate in spiced vinegar and claret wine. Marinate for at least an hour. While all this is going on (the marination, etc.), mince and mince good the following vegetables: a green pepper, an onion, a lot of parsley, and some celery. Now, girls, keep the vegetables separate.

Here's a slight trick for looks only, but they look swell if you can do this. Arrange the shrimp in individual shells for baking. There is a large half shell made for baking

Stolen Recipe Section!

that is perfect for this deal, especially for buffet serving. However, a large baking dish may be used.

Before the baking starts, regardless of which "baker-inner" you use, sprinkle about a tablespoon of *each* minced vegetable over the shrimp, season well, and add a little of the spice vinegar and claret over the top. Then re-top generously with minced parsley and cracker crumbs. Now, lastly, cover this well with melted butter, then brown in a hot oven. Doesn't take long to brown same, so don't go to another part of the house and start doing something you should have done the day before. Watch this dish. An important secret is to be *sure* the dish is well covered with parsley while baking.

Ham "Cops" Ham

Many people steal—many people get caught. I hope I don't because I stole this recipe from a lady in Alaska . . . she had stolen it from her husband and it turned out her husband was a policeman in Ketchikan, Alaska. Her name was Dollie—but at least, publicly, I frankly admit I copped something from a cop's wife. Old Vincent Hamling (Officer Hamling, that is).

To make this thing, of course, the first thing you have to have is a ham. Got it? Goody. Now this next trick is good if you can do it, and you can if you take your time.

Skin the fat off the ham in one piece. Then, put it gently to one side. Now, score the top of the skinned ham. *(I learned what scoring was on a typewriter. When scored, the top of the ham will look like this:* ########.*)* Now put cloves in opposite corners of the scores. Then split a big clove of garlic and rub gently over the entire ham. Now rub brown sugar lightly all over the ham. Y'know, it might be easier to put the cloves in later. Ya. Now put the cloves in. Then cover this whole business with sliced or crushed pineapple. Not too much, but be sure it's going to stick on top. Do you remember that big piece of fat you skinned off a while ago? Lay it over the ham that you have done all this stuff to. Gently. Anchor it well with toothpicks so she'll stick in place. Bake this in about a 350° oven, 35 minutes to the pound. Baste it frequently. I wonder where that cop stole that from, but at least after you try this you'll admit there's a mighty good thief.

Ribzzzzzz

This is a hotsy-totsy recipe for ribs. I stole it from Cora Pearson, and it's one reason her husband, Fort, is so fat. He's a radio announcer. This is a trick way to have barbecued spareribs inside and no trouble. I not only stole the recipe, but the night I had them I stole most of them. So, beware of thieves at your home.

Stolen Recipe Section!

Get yourself about 4 or 5 pounds of lean pork ribs. Slap 'em in a roaster big enough to spread them out a bit. Salt and pepper, then pour over this little group of hog at least ¾ to full bottle of good, sweet catsup. Cover all this with Worcestershire, which will be up to your and your kinfolks' taste as to quantity. Put in the oven and if the gas or light bill is paid, turn it on. About 300° is okay. Let 'em go a while, then keep turning them until done. I know a lot of you will cheat and put more junk in the roaster, but I sure know this way will work.

Pearl's Peachy Puffy Soufflé

There's a charming lady and hostess in Oak Park, Illinois, and her name is Pearl Wade. Her husband owns an advertising agency by the same name. (Without the Pearl, of course.) Now they made the error of asking me out to their house and served this soufflé. I nearly lost their friendship and my figure by eating so much of it. Wait and see how this turns out and you'll know what I mean by good:

Take 2½ cups of tomato purée, 7½ tablespoons of butter, 7½ tablespoons of flour, 2½ cups of grated cheese, cook in a double boiler for about 20 minutes and cool. Bust and separate 7 eggs and add well-beaten yolks (the yellow part) to mixture, then fold in stiffly beaten whites.

Put in a large casserole or reasonable facsimile and bake it in a slow oven in a pan of water for an hour and a quarter. This will quiet from 10 to 12 souls, or if you're mathematical, divide everything in two.

Pickled Rolled Steak

Mildred Morgan, former singer, dancer, swimming instructor, amateur nurse, secretary, personnel manager, and at present manager of her husband, Jim Morgan, can also cook. One night at their house for dinner, Millie stooped over, caught her pinz niz on something, and was near-sighted for two hours, so I absconded with the following:

Get 2 pounds of round steak, cut very thin. Carefully cut in squares about 4 inches square, these are to be rolled later. Now, then, on each square, at one end put a strip of bacon, thin slice of onion, wedge-shaped, thin slice of garlic pickle. Roll these squares and tie with string two places near the ends. Flour and brown in oil, in a Dutch oven. When fully browned, add ½ to a cup of water, put the lid on, and steam until done. Fifteen minutes before serving add about ½ cup of cooking sherry. Do not salt this too much. These are awful cute and awful good. The blending of the flavors in steaming is the secret.

Squab Super Chief

This was stolen first by the steward, Bert Hertl, from the chef, Henry C. Berard, and in talking about it I jotted it down on the back of an old bill of fare—leaving the Super Chief with it safely tucked in my shoe:

Cook a young squab in a casserole and garnish with truffles, stuffed olives, and fresh mushroom sauce made of mushrooms, cognac, Madeira wine, and cream. This sauce has to be made by taste, by guess, and by smell. They said it depended on how much you want, how thick you want it, or if you want it. Good luck. They're swell guys, anyway.

Burrage Porrage

Alice Burrage is a career girl, and people seldom think they can cook—career girls often think that people don't think of career girls ever, but I think this career girl's porrage is tops:

Take 1 can of tomato soup and 1 can of pea soup, put in a double boiler, and dilute with milk. When it is coming along but not too hot, add a desired amount of lobster or crab meat. You can judge the amount to suit yourself. Leave this on the stove about 40 minutes with a little salt and pepper. The last 10 minutes add about 2 jiggers of cooking sherry and you've got it. Here's to the career girls and your career with Burrage Porrage.

Salad Philly

Philly, as you know, is short for Philadelphia, and when in that town and you think of good things to eat, you think of the good Palumbo boys and their places. The "Chief" and Frank are too nice to actually steal from, so I came right out and mooched this one from the Maitre d' of the C. and R. Club, whose name is Vito Guala. These proportions are for one salad:

In a mixing bowl, put 2 teaspoons of A-1 sauce, 1 teaspoon of Lea and Perrins, 4 tablespoons of sweet catsup, 4 tablespoons pure olive oil, and 1 teaspoon of vinegar. Mix thoroughly and add to well-drained salad greens. There's a salad and dressing that's plumb good and should make Palumbos proud.

Deep South Ribs

We have a young lady who is a big help around the house. Her name is Alberta Talbot. One of her compliments was that "when you cook you don't mess up the kitchen like most folks." Her biggest insult was the day

Stolen Recipe Section! 67

I was experimenting on making a new style chocolate cake. I asked her to look at it in the oven, and her insult was, "Mr. Jack, that don't look like a cake, it looks like a chocolate malted milk." Hmmm. To turn the tables on sister Talbot I have sneaked from her this pantry pleasantry.

Fry 2 pounds of pork ribs in enough fat until they are brown. Take them out and keep them warm. Now chop up a large onion, a bell pepper, 1 small pod of garlic, and fry these together in the rib fat. In a casserole pour a #2 can of corn, pour over this the onion, pepper, and garlic that's been fried. Lay the cooked ribs on top of this and pour over all 1 can of tomato sauce. Shades of real cookin', that's it. What that won't do to your reputation.

Corny Stuffin'

I'm practically a second time loser with Alberta on this one, but it's so good and different I must steal it and, under cover of this culinary chronicle, excuse myself by the fact it's worth swiping.

Boil some giblets of the fowl at hand until very tender. Now toast a loaf of white bread and when toasted tear it up and add it to a pan (medium size) of *corn* bread. Chop up 2 large onions, a bell pepper, small pod of garlic, and fry them together. . . . Add this to the chopped giblets and stock and mix with the bread mixture. Season this to taste and you've got a "stuffin'" that when you stuff whatever you're gonna stuff, you'll be glad you stuffed it with this stuff.

Marcelled Broccoli

This must be called Marcelled because the gent from which I stole this wonderful dish is actually named Marcel. The whole cognomen is Marcel Lamaze—maitre d' at the world-famous Earl Carroll Theatre Restaurant in Hollywood. He's a nice guy, short, fat, and less hair than I have, and I know he learned all he knows about maitre d'ing from his mother in New York. I know her and like her very much, and she's a wonderful cook—*but* for once instead of telling chefs what to do, Marcel actually made this broccoli dish which made me once again abandon my natural honesty and kidnap the idea. Away we go.

First we take a bunch of fresh broccoli, cut off the large leaves, and peel off the woody outer skin of the main stem. Boil this whole in salted water until tender. Drain and leave on fire a moment until dry. Place this on a baking platter and forget it for the moment. Now in a pan put 1 tablespoon of butter and 2 finely chopped challots, ½ cup of cream, and 1 tablespoon of sweet cooking sherry. Then add 1 tablespoon of grated cheese,

2 pinches of paprika, season with salt and pepper, then let it come to a slight boil. Pour over the broccoli. Now mix 1 tablespoon of bread crumbs, 1 tablespoon of grated cheese, a small amount of chopped parsley, and sprinkle over the broccoli and place in a preheated oven (moderate) for about 10 minutes. There you have it, friends and neighbors, and it is delicious. Broccoli seems to be overlooked too much as people usually just boil it, butter it, and serve it. Try this and it will glorify the broccoli as Earl Carroll has girls and Marcel has food. My best to you and your broccoli.

Dentist's Dutch Oven

I have no shame or compunction about stealing this recipe. This guy has stolen most of my teeth, so why wouldn't I at least take something from him? I'm sure I'm perhaps the only person in the world that gets scared when going to a dentist. This guy took one look at me the first time and instead of talking teeth started talking about pleasant things and all of a sudden we were talking about cooking and all of another sudden my tooth was out. He kept the tooth and I kept the recipe, and his professional card which reads "J. Lorenz Jones, Exodontist" means, I guess, he is a mighty good tooth bandit. Speaking of teeth (I shudder), here is a tempting, toothsome tidbit.

Once again the Dutch oven. In it braise 2½ or 3 pounds of ends and trimmings of meat with its own fat. Peel and quarter about half a dozen potatoes and simmer them for ½ hour. Then add them to the meat along with 3 medium fresh onions quartered, one chopped clove of garlic, season with salt and pepper and a big slurp of heavy cooking sherry. Cover and simmer this whole thing for at least 2 hours. This is also a wonderful outdoor dish over a pit of coals in a barbecue, or a regular wood fire and grate on a camping trip.

Now here's what the D.D.S. also told me about the above. Most anything around they put in, like apples, etc. He told me that once he had some leftover mince pie and put that in too. Now you can believe that or not —but if you mincepie it up a bit and it doesn't seem to taste quite right, write J. Lorenz, not me. It was his idea, not mine. Happy extractions to you all.

Dude Ranch Dandy

Lots of you folks have never gone to a dude ranch and I hadn't either until this one time my wife talked me into it. She likes horses and outdoor life, and I don't mind it, but I was afraid of all the cowboys not having guitars, and no moonlight nights on the prairie, and also not being a rider, I was afraid they'd give me a bronc to bust (or he'd bust me). Well, we went up there anyway (does everybody's wife always win out? Ha, as if I

Stolen Recipe Section! 71

didn't know) and it was wonderful. The hostess on the dude ranch was a Dorothy Warren who looked a little like a horsewoman in costume but was as cute as a colt (small). Now she could ride, sing, dance, and how she could cook. . . . Lots of talent in Dorothy. I wrangled this recipe from the young cowgal who was the cutie of the Chuck Wagon!

This is a coffee cake special like. First you cream ½ cup of sugar and 2 tablespoons of shortening. Then add the yolk of 1 egg and stir around some. Now add 1 cup of milk and 2 cups of flour alternately, then sneak in 2 teaspoons of baking powder, all through the above. Beat ingredients together well and then add white of the egg beaten stiffly. Pour in greased baking pan and proceed like this:

Topping comes next, naturally. Cream ½ cup of brown sugar and 2 tablespoons of butter, a little cinnamon, and spread this over the top, and then add some chopped walnuts or pecans. Slap in a moderate oven and bake for about 45 minutes.

NOTE: *If you're an old hand at cooking, sift dry ingredients together, but a lot of novices don't do that right. Now dood this Dude good and it will be.*

Schloterbeck Special

Every hotel has a manager and the Hollywood Plaza had theirs. He's a wonderful man, a great host, and a thwarted cook. He, too, is a man with the most misspelled name in the country. It's Johnny (that's easy) Slaughterback, Slotterberger, Schlitterstein, or Schloterbeck. I honestly don't know, and I don't think he nor his wife Dorothy know. But I do know this Special is a dish fit for anyone, name or no name. Johnny says you do this:

For four get about 1½ pounds of top sirloin, and when you are ready to start, cube it. As you are cubing, take some grease and get it hot, then dice about ¼ Spanish onion and put in grease to lightly brown. By then the beef is cubed, so add with salt and ground pepper and brown that. Now add about 2 tablespoons of tomato juice and tomato paste each, with a dash of good sweet chili sauce. While this is simmering (covered), peel and thinly slice lengthwise a few potatoes. When meat is brownish add this, with ½ cup of water, and let the whole thing simmer some more. Then prepare a gravy made of cold water, flour, Maggi, one bay leaf, a pinch of cayenne, Worcestershire, steak sauce, and salt and pepper. Take ½ of a lemon rind and grate it very fine, a dash of garlic salt, and mix this thoroughly. When potatoes look about two-thirds done, pour this gravy (cold) over the meat mixture and let it simmer some more.

Stolen Recipe Section!

Don't cook too fast, just easy as she goes, and you'll end up with something really. Serve over toasted rolls with melted cheese or over mashed vegetables. This I can recommend and it came directly from my friend Slaughterbeck. I happen to know he stole it from one of his bellboys, but I won't tell.

Good "spuds" is good.

CHAPTER FIVE

THE POTATO PATCH

A potato is a potato even if it's called a spud. And good "spuds" is good. People work for hours and hours and sometimes days to make an elaborate meal. Come potato time and they simply bake, boil, brown, or bust out with a potato compilation that is common and usual. Why not all of us trip lightly to that grand old culinary city of "Spudville," and look around for the better type of potato eating. I repeat, a potato is a potato, but with a pinch of this, a dash of that, a squirt of this and a swish of that, it turns into a big feature of the eatin' meetin'. So join me with the bunches of squirts, swish, dash and pinches of thisa's and thata's, and learn to enjoy good old "Spudville." All aboard!!!

Potato Tinero

For them that's lazy (like most of us) let's stay lazy right now. "Tinero" is only fancy talk for tin can. Ya ever try canned potatoes? I never had either until I was up in the mountains one day and the lady of the house was cooking a batch of stuff for all of us (and we were hungry). About the time things began smelling like they were ready to eat, she yelled in a loud voice, "How about potatoes?" Everyone said, "No, it'll take too long. Skip 'em!" She yelled back with a lady-like "Phooey," grabbed her trusty can opener, used same and poured the spuds, juice and all, in a pan on top the stove. Added a bit of cream, put up some cheese (American), salt and pepper, het them a little, stirred them once or twice, and then het them some more. By the time the rest of the meal was done so were the canned, creamed, cheesed potatoes, and the only catch was we had to ruin her eating dinner so she would go make some more. They were that good, believe me. Now, honestly, I should have ended this chapter on the Potato Patch with the above, 'cause now you probably will do this all the time and not read the rest of it. Better glance on, tho', even if it's just for laughs.

The Ball of the Potato

Shall we all quit frowning on the good old-fashioned boiled potato long enough to boil a few? Peeling and boiling is a thing that we have all been doing for years. It's easy and a thing that makes new brides think they are a success in this art of cooking. But to carry on a bit farther with these boiled beauties, and still not overtax patience or luck at not burning in the boiling, let's just do this. Mash them up good and mashed, salt, pepper, and then add some milk and butter to make a right good stiff batter or mixture. Now take your lily-white hands and mold this mixture in balls. Let's say good golf-ball size (and let's say no more about golf either. I quit). Now melt some more butter and roll the potato balls in it, then in crushed corn flakes. Slap them in the refrigerator or Servel or what have you and go about your business. When your business is attended to, and ½ hour before you want to serve them, place in a buttered pan and heat through in a moderate oven. This has taken a lot longer to write than it will to do, 'cause I had to remember what the man did (I got this from a he, not a she).

Seven Come Eleven Potatoes

Now herein you'll find a quick and efficient potato business that comes out swell—7 come 11, of course, means dice. So dice some fresh whites, put them in a pot with a tight cover, and add just a little water. Let them get fairly well cooked and the water almost cooked away. Then add enough half and half cream to almost cover them. Put in a good big hunk of butter, salt and pepper, and then let them cook. This will be a creamed potato dish in less time than you imagine. After you use this dish once, you'll repeat and repeat. If you've made too much the first time, reheat and reheat—it works. We had this for dinner once at the home of a drama critic. The next morning for breakfast, his wife added a little cream and butter, warmed them good, and then browned them in a skillet. Some kind of good spuds, and no pain in the making either for dinner that night or the refixing in the A.M. They, as you can see, will fit in with practically any menu, both night and morning. *Good!*

Potato Scaloopie

I have often wondered why this type potato is called scalloped. A scallop is a form of seafood. The method of cooking is different, yet for generations they have called this potato job scalloped. Someday I may find out, but I still like this style spud in spite of its misnomer. (Me wife can do a bit of artistry on this too, and so can you.) Shall we try? Let's!!!

In a glass baking dish, slice a layer of fresh white potatoes sliced paper thin, on top of said layer sift a bit of flour, then sprinkle a bit of American cheese—next layer the same except on this one salt a bit and add some ground fresh black pepper. Keep this up until dish is full (alternating as above). When dish is full, pour over enough good milk to almost cover. Slice cheese over top and put in oven in a pan. This is liable to run over so be sure and put a pan under it. Cook in a moderate oven for about 1½ hours. There will be a blend of flavor here (and please, black freshly ground pepper) that is great.

P.S. If the potatoes are not sliced paper thin, the dish is likely to become gummy and that's not so good. Do like I said above and it is good (if you like it).

Bailey Chips

Ha! This is so easy, simple, and sumptuous, I'm most ashamed to put it down, but I will, and you'll hate me because you didn't think of it first. Take several potatoes that are not too large. Slice them vertical to about the size of a quarter (two-bit pieces). If your batch of spuds are large, pare them down to size wanted (saving the rest for slivery julienne). When all the two-bit discs are ready, put them in deep fat, with a bit of salt later, and serve. You know about de-greasing them on paper towels, I guess, and keep the little devils warm and they will then be servable nice and crisp like. Try this with a steak some time and they beat the socks off those pithy homemade French fries. Excellent with eggs of a morning, too. Ah yes—good with anything almost except potato salad.

Patty-Cake Potatoes

I can never remember not making too big a batch of mashed potatoes. Always, always have some left over. Now don't get mad like I did so many times and dump them out. My wife caught me doing it and said to me something I can't print. She carefully and patiently explained to me the Montana Method of using mashed leftovers. As always, the little woman was *half* right. Then *I* added something and we came up with this likeable leftover.

Grate a little onion and chop fine some parsley. Salt and pepper. Mix well until blended. Then you well-flour each hand (yours). Make patty-cakes of mashed potatoes, with the cold leftovers that is, and dip in grated onion and parsley plate. Brown patties in very hot beef drippings or leftover bacon grease. By using a pancake turner carefully, they will not break apart, and by golly they will taste like something you are sorry that you didn't have before. This doesn't take long, as you can see, so don't do the patty-cake routine and then monkey around with something else. Monkey around first and do this last, just before serving.

I just thought of something here for breakfast, going over the above patty-cake. If'n you hanker for a slick breakfast dish, why not toast some bread, in a toaster, then put it in the top of a modern oven to melba-type it, poach an egg per customer (in Boston I learned they are not called poached but "dropped," or as they say, drapped eggs). Toast first, patty next, poach or drap next, then a crisp piece of bacon over all. Hey—I may

The Potato Patch 81

go try that now, sounds good enough to eat. Here I go. Yoweeeee.

Sweet Spudatoes . . .

Not yams, but good old country sweet potatoes. Boil them in skins until done, peel and put them in a glass baking dish. Dash of rich cream, stir in plenty of fresh walnuts, lots of little butter hunks, and stir again. Then smooth out the top and fully blanket with bits of marshmallow. Bake in a moderate oven for enough time to brown the marshmallows. Some place in this volume of vittles I've told you about cutting marshmallows with scissors and water. So many people used canned candied yams (they're good) but I still stick with this job using fresh well-raised sweet potatoes. I'd been eating yams for years, but a woman in Beatrice, Nebraska, made this deal and I've been cooking and raving about it ever since. Think how this would taste with ham.

Baked Potato Spinochi

Once upon a time someone told me baked potatoes were *not* fattening. Well, I like baked potatoes, and like so many of us, I don't like getting fatter. Now no one wants to get fat and most "no one" will eat spinach...but here's something that will make non-spinachers and non-fatters get along and it's all in the same recipe. Nine times out of nine they don't know what's happened. We know (if you read and try this) but don't tell them. I had it pulled on me once, in a home I trusted. I didn't gain an ounce but did surely enjoy this conglomeration.

The first thing you do is sneak up on 3 or 4 nice large baking potatoes. Wash them and bake them (first rubbing their healthy skins with bacon grease or Crisco). Bake in a hot oven for 1 hour or until done. While this baking process is going on, drain a can of spinach and chop it up fine. Season it with grated onion, salt, pepper, and celery salt. Now, when the baking is baked with the potatoes, take them out and cut in half lengthwise. Scoop out the pulp and whip it until fluffy. Add a couple of good-sized hunks of butter, some hot cream or milk, and season with salt and pepper. (((Oh! Oh!))) I nearly forgot to tell you that just before the potatoes are done, warm that spinach thing above—don't get it too hot, just warm it a bit. Now we proceed. Mix the spinach mixture and the hot scooped potato pulp together and put back into the baked potato shells. Now cover each potato shell with finely chopped bacon, put in moderate oven and bake until bacon is brown and the potato part is well browned. If someone's sick or someone's well, this Spinochi dish will taste real swell.

The Potato Patch

Jack's Juliennes

This number is good for breakfast, brunch, dinner, or even a midnight snacker, and takes such a little time you can run it in without losing friends, guests, or face. As the merry mad gang played the pianos (we have two), victrola or radio, I would slip to our kitchen and do this: add an egg apiece or maybe an old leftover wienie, but whatever you have on hand whip up the Jack Julienne with it. Like this here:

Peel 6 medium-sized raw potatoes, slice lengthwise, and cut into thin strips. Mess up about 6 strips of bacon into very small bits and fry the bacon for just a moment or two in a hot skillet. Now dump in the potato strips and mix around with the frying bacon. Take a spatula (big word for pancake turner) and flatten this whole batch into a solid mass. Then cook for 10 minutes, and carefully turn it on its little back and cook for 15 minutes on that side. Best cover the skillet, and peek quite often lest potatoes burn. Remove to a hot platter and shove it at the eaters, with whatever you're going to use with it. A good idea is to pour the drippings from the pan over it before serving, and I always like to ring it with fresh green onions. This will handle about half a dozen people and I have found that a bowl (or bottle) of good sweet chili sauce disappears at the same time. Speaking of chili sauce (and we weren't), if you put it in a bowl fancy like they think it's something special, but if you just put it on in the bottle they know what it is and you can have some left for the next day—in case that's your last bottle. Cheer up. Everyone runs out of things all the time.

Kartoffel Klosse
(Potato balls supreme)

Let us suppose you have time to fuss around a bit with some spuds. Things in the oven are coming along swell, things on top the stove are doing fine, and you find yourself with a little extra time. I learned that if you can still stand up from non-fatigue, you can use this time to make a dashing hit by working on some other dish to go with your dinner. If you are so tired you have to sit down, stay a second and put on 6 medium potatoes in their jackets and cook them (*boil*). When done, peel and put the little fellers through a ricer. Then spread out on a clean towel to dry out the moisture. Place in a large bowl and sprinkle in a couple of level teaspoons of salt, then make a valley or hollow and break into this 2 eggs. Sift in ¾ cup of flour, and add ½ cup of bread crumbs and ¼ teaspoon of nutmeg. Smash and work this all up together, and then put on bread board and knead well until you can make them into dry balls. Now make up a series of small potato balls and drop into boiling water (salted). When the potato balls come bubbling to the top let 'em go for another 3 or 4 minutes. Sneak one out then and

The Potato Patch 85

test it by cutting it in half—if the center is dry (not soggy) get them out of the water with a wire spoon. Don't boil them too long or the little devils will fall apart or become awful squiggy. The next thing to do is to use your natural gravy from whatever you are cooking to pour over these. Serve them on a platter surrounding the meat and vegetables, with gravy over same and a bit of paprika, for to make it pretty. Incidentally, these Potato Balls Supreme are supreme with Sauerbraten or Hassenpfeffer. You'll find them listed in another part of this tome (and probably under a different name) but, don't ever overlook Kartoffel Klosse.

Nutty Potato Croquettes

There is something about a croquette type thing, no matter what it is, that makes it look and seemingly taste better. Say on a plate of something light in the way of meat, slap a couple of these croquette jobs and they'll go along with the meal fancy like. When I first had these I said, what kind of cereal did you roll the potato balls in, and the lady of the house simply said, *nuts*! Boil and smash up enough white potatoes to make about 4 or 5 cupfuls. Make them into small croquette shapes and let them cool. When you are ready to cook them again, dip them in a beaten egg that has had a spoonful or two of water added. Now grind, crush, and pulverize some fresh peanuts. Roll the croquettes in the ground, crushed, and pulverized peanuts and fry same in deep fat. Drain them on a paper towel or something and serve them at once. I hastily add that anyone not liking nutty Potato Croqs is really nutty.

Ah Gratin Ah

Because this dish has a foreign name on most menus, most people at home leave it off most menus. Now I learned from a guy once how to make these Au Gratoon things and it was so simple it made me feel simpler. Here's what: boil yourself several potatoes, slice or cube them. Make a fairly thin cream sauce with a lot of cheese in it in a double boiler. Take your little sliced or diced numbers, put in a glass baking dish, make a layer or so, salt and grind on some fresh black pepper, ease a little of the cheesed cream sauce over it, and then carry on till the dish is full. Sneak a few more hunks of cheese over the top and then pour the rest of the sauce over the whole shebuddle. Bake until well baked, but not baked enough to be too baked. Ah, yes, Ah Gratin—Ahhhh!

Chili Potatoes

Now we have a spud dish that should be called a bachelor's best, but shes as well as hes can run this up. It's almost a meal, in fact, with a big tossed salad it is a meal. A meal that's real, tempting, and good. Also easy.

The Potato Patch

What more can any of us cooks want? Try this and the only want you'll have is to want some more. This I learned from a male ballet dancer. He was a swell dancer and so was this Chili Potato dish.

For as many people as you're feeding bake as many potatoes. Whilst they are baking, sauté lightly some fresh ground round or sirloin. When it is a light brown, add some tomato paste (just a little), some grated onion, chili powder (a dash), and salt and pepper. When baked potatoes are baked, carefully halve them and scoop out spuds, mix with meat, tomato mixture, and stir around. Be careful the meat business isn't too greasy. Now when this is thoroughly mixed, refill the baked potato skins and rebake for about 10 minutes. As I said, toss a salad, toss on the spuds (if you want to be extra-fancy, put a crisp slice of bacon over each spud), serve, and take bows for the rest of the evening.

Real New Potato Zeal

In thinking of new potatoes (if anyone thinks of new potatoes much) most cooks say, "New potatoes? Certainly I know how to use them. Fresh peas and cream sauce—how else?" I'll tell you how else right this very minute. Ready, the moment is here. Well-scrape a couple or 3 pounds of new potatoes. Now rind a lemon, and while you are rinding the lemon melt about ¼ cup of butter, stir in some flour (just a wee pinch), add salt and pepper and the lemon rind grated. Cook this for about 1½ minutes, and then pour over the potatoes and let them heat in the mixture, but do not boil. Now stir in a teaspoon of chopped chives and the juice of 1 lemon. Can't you just imagine what that will do to a meal, and believe me it will. I kinda didn't want to try it at first, but I'm glad I did. It makes me glad I got glad and now you get glad like I got glad. (New potatoes and creamed peas indeed. Ha!)

Potato Puffers

An old method, tried and true, but a real fine deviation of the run of the mill potatoes. Easy, quick, and pretty. Simply boil and smash enough potatoes to make a cupful. Add the yolks of two eggs beaten quite well. Now ya sift 1 cup of flour and 1 teaspoon of baking powder and add to the potato mixture alternately with 1 cup of milk. Next you fold in the egg white beaten stiff with a pinch of salt. Get some deep fat going good and drop in potato mixture in small portions from a teaspoon. Cook until they are brown and puffed up. Drain on paper and serve. Then it'll be your turn to puff up.

*And now we come to the end of a chapter,
Full of spuds and a little laughter.
So not in the words of Socrates or Plato—
"Never underestimate the glories of a well
    fixed potato."*

He *has to have a special dish!*

CHAPTER SIX

EASY ON THE TUMMY

In every household there is either someone sick, young, old, too fat, too skinny, too something or other, and they always have to have a special dish. Meatless, starchless, tasteless, or something. Here then are some slap-happy things to fit practically any of these characters. Funny thing is that most of them are pretty darn good.

Corn Meal Phfft

This is an awful lot better than it sounds, so sick or well try it sometime. Get 3 cups of milk boiling and then put in ¼ cup of yellow corn meal. Let this boil about 15 minutes, then whisk in 3 teaspoons of fresh butter. Allow this to cool a little. While this junk is cooling a little, whip 4 egg yolks to lemon yellow. Add these to above and then beat the 4 egg whites until they're stiff. Fold 'em in. Now ya pour this whole bunch of stuff into a buttered casserole. Set the casserole et. al. in a pan of hot water and cook in a low oven. Now look out, kid, you don't get the oven too hot, 'cause you don't want the water in the pan to boil. Test it like any cake or mush to find out when it's done, then hurry up and serve it before it gets cold. Getting cold makes this Phfft very sad to behold and eat. Serve it either with maple syrup or with cheese sauce.

Walnut Maindisher

Get a load of this beauty for a meatless meal. First you crumb up 1 cup of zwieback. Then pour a cup of milk, and pour ¾ of the cup of milk over the zwieback. Let this stand while you make a sort of sauce. Cook 3 tablespoons of minced onions with a tablespoon of minced parsley and 1½ teaspoons of melted butter. Cook this until tender, but *not* brown. Stir in 1 tablespoon of flour and when frothy add the rest of the milk. When this stuff all thickens up nice like, pour in a slightly beaten egg, then next stir in ½ cup of ground walnuts and some salt. Oh dear, I forgot to tell you to steam 1 cup of rice. Don't forget to steam the rice so that by now it will be steamed. Now that you have the steamed rice, fold it in with a fork, then slap this whole business in a loaf pan, shove it in the oven for about 45 minutes at 375°. This will be moist inside and have a crisp brown crush—or else you did something wrong. Don't forget to steam the rice first. Sorry I forgot.

Eggs Sickbed

When most folks feel kinda rotten, but think they should eat something, they whip up a "graveyard" stew. Y'know that's boiling some milk, adding a bit of butter and salt and pepper, then dumping it over some toast. Now if you're not too sick and can stand the thought of an egg or two, do this.

Get a pan of cream (or half and half). Slowly boil it adding butter, salt, and pepper. When it is boiling drop in two eggs and turn the fire off. Make some toast and when the eggs are done (in about 2 or 3 minutes) pour this over the toast. If you are rugged enough, a couple slices of crisp bacon goes keen with this. After you eat this you'll probably want to get upset again so you can have some more. I've tried it when I was well and it still tastes good.

P.S. In case you didn't know it, the above is known in classy joints as "Eggs Vienna." Of course in those places it usually costs a lot of money—so make it at home.

Egg Noggin

Mothers and nurses and such through the ages have been trying to get people to drink eggnogs. They get tiresome, turned down, and quite often the prospects for these eggnogs get sore. Now here's a trick I learned and by George I drink 'em real often. Once when my mother was sick I suggested this concoction, and I'm sure that's what put her on her feet. Take a look at this.

In a big glass fill it half full of fresh strained orange juice. Then fill it up with homogenized milk. Pour this into a mixing bowl, bust an egg in it, and drip in just a very little crushed ice. Mix this well either in a whirling gadget or old-fashioned egg beater. Serve it right away with salted crackers. Better not tell anyone there's an egg in it or they might squawk. If they don't know it they'll never catch on.

A Spinach Slicker

Probably the vittle that draws more turned-up noses in the world is spinach. Me included. But one day I messed around with a can of the stuff and now I like it and people who didn't like spinach at all eat it. Try it once and you'll do it again.

Fry a couple hunks of bacon crisp. Then in a glass baking dish pour the spinach, juice and all. Crumble the crisp bacon in, add a healthy dash of cider vinegar, one raw egg, a shot of Heinz 57 sauce (good shot), dash of tabasco, Worcestershire, salt and pepper. In the palm of your hands crush quite a few fresh crackers and dump

Easy on the Tummy

them in. Mix this thoroughly and then sprinkle some good old American cheese all over the top. Don't be stingy now, use plenty of cheese. Bake this till it looks done and the cheese is melted, serve it, and perhaps you'll never hear your family cuss spinach again.

Thought I might tell you that in dishes like the above with a lot of different things in it, I find that if you stir it after each addition, then again when all the junk's in it, the overall result of the dish is much better. You can't stir stuff too much in this sort of dish—but you can stir it too hard. Stir gently, but often. You're welcome.

Where did that come from?

CHAPTER SEVEN

EGG EDIBILITIES

A 3-In-1 Omelet

I should like to make an urgent plea here and now that cooks quit putting all their "eggs in one skillet." Most people in thinking of eggs simply worry about them being fried sunny side up, basted lightly, or boiled. Please, let us band together, make use of these following "Symphonies of Hen Fruit," and once again respect will be due where respect is due. *I salute you oh mighty egg.* (I should, I've laid plenty of them in show business and radio.)

The gay little 3-in-1 is basically bacon, potato, and eggs. The most successful ratio is 1 slice of bacon (cut up) to ½ raw potato to 2 eggs. Figure out how many mouths to feed and multiply the above by each mug. Now then, sizzle the bacon until crisp, remove from fat, and slap in the spuds that you're supposed to have diced. Fry them slow like, until they're done. Mess up the quota of eggs you want, chop up a little parsley, and add both this and the bacon. Then dump over the spuds and cook until their bottom is browned. Put under the broiler until top is like you like it. Fold—serve—eat it now. wow!!!

A Poaching Production

This little gem might sound troublesome, but stick it out once and you'll tackle it again:

First thing is to whip up a medium cream sauce, and for each cup of it add 2 beaten egg yolks, ½ cup of grated cheese, and a dash of cooking sherry. Season with salt and pepper. Keep it hot while you skip to the next department of this production. Right this very minute trim and sauté in butter the desired number of pieces of toast you'll be needing. Put them on a serving platter you can keep warm (and do so). Cover each slice with a piece of boiled ham that's been slightly sautéed. If you want to, put a slice of friend tomato on the ham (never cared for that myself). Poach as many eggs as you have people to serve. Don't worry, they'll want seconds. Incidentally, did you know that when poaching eggs, if you pour in a little vinegar it helps keep the eggs from busting. After poaching has been accomplished to your satisfaction, gently place one on each toast mound (that you have kept warm) and then pour the cream sauce (that you have kept warm) *around* them, but do not cover the eggs (that you have kept warm). This dish will do your heart good (that you have kept warm).

Egg Bread Crumb Batch
(for a laff repeat that three times fast)

Here's a little number that is surprisingly swell, swift, and sensational. Well, it's good and easy anyway:

Chop up a couple slices of bacon (fine) or grind up 4 or 5 tablespoons of raw ham. Fry slowly, and when it's nearly cooked add ½ cup of *fresh* bread crumbs. Keep on frying until the meat and crumbs are a light brown. Stir this all the time, or you'll be sorry. Now whap thunder out of 4 eggs in ⅓ cup of milk. (I use half and half when my wife isn't looking). Pour this mixture over the meat and crumbs and stir until the eggs are cooked. If you are inclined to be skimpy you can serve about four with this. Thot I'd run that in as fair warning.

Oiled Eggs

Turneth not thy nose up, 'till you read this and try it. Please:

Sauté your eggs in olive oil until the eggs become crisp and brown around their little edges. Serve with tomato or Spanish sauce. When you try it you may quote me as saying, "Ha ha. I told you so!"

The Mushroom and the Egg

There's so much stuff goes in this "Operation Egg" I best list the contents first before we all get so mixed up it never will come out even. Here 'tis:

2 tablespoons butter, ½ pound mushrooms, 2 tablespoons flour, 2 cups chicken broth, 3 tablespoons thick cream or evaporated milk, ½ teaspoon chopped onion, tablespoon (1) chopped parsley, salt and pepper, naturally eggs—6 of 'em. Now to stand by for sprinkling over the top purposes: 2 tablespoons of melted butter and grated Parmesan cheese. (That cheese I can neither pronounce nor spell.) Now here we go, kids. Melt the first butter in a pan and sauté the mushrooms. When browned and squishy enough for ya, stir in the flour and blend the dickens out of it. Add broth, cream, onion and parsley, season with salt and pepper, and cook, stir, and cook until it's smooth. Pour this sauce into a flatbottomed baking dish, then ease the eggs in the dish, but on the surface—don't bury the poor things. Take the rest of your butter and that high sounding cheese and pour and sprinkle (in the order mentioned) over the top. Bake in a medium oven until eggs are cooked. Quite a dish, eh? Humph. And people scoff at egg dishes.

Scramble Special

'Tisn't really special at all:

Do it your own way but add a teaspoon of grated onion, a shot of tabasco, and a drop or two of Worcestershire. Ever try scrambling in a buttered double boiler? The slower you scramble the eggs the faster the boarders scramble to the table.

The Aloof Omelet

In the case of the "Aloof Omelet," aloof literally translated means a-loaf, but I didn't want to scare you with that name, because you cannot loaf and make this baby come out right. All right, hang on to your front burners, 'cause here we go:

Cut 4 slices of toast in small cubes and sauté in 3 tablespoons of butter with 2 tablespoons of minced parsley and chopped green onions or shallots. Having done this, put same aside for the nonce. Beat lots of eggs (maybe a dozen) in a bowl, add salt and pepper to taste, and ¼ cup of heavy cream. Add some more butter to the skillet, pour egg mixture in, and cook 'er slow. (Low flame that is.) Keep lifting the cooked eggs away from side of skillet and let center ooze over and get set. When about half cooked, add crouton mixture, then cover this whole thing with grated cheddar cheese. Finish cooking and fold over; remove to heated platter and slice into servings. Be sure not to over-cook, as its aloofness is aloofer when not too firm. How about the above for flavor? Great for luncheons, dinners, breakfast, Sunday suppers, after-theatre parties. Not so good for tea time. Or maybe it is.

Chinese Egg Foo Yong

Here's a surprise package that most people are scared to try, but be of good cheer. This always results in, "Did you really make this? Hmmm, let me have the recipe. Oh, I'll bet you brought it home from a Chinese restaurant and reheated it." You check on the results at your table so's it won't make me out a liar. Before I forget it, most people shy at so many dishes fearing they can't get the junk to put in it. Not so in most cases, but it takes a bit of shopping and sharp-eyed friends on the outlook. Now back to cooking:

Lightly beat 4 eggs with a fork in a large mixing bowl, then stir in the following: One cup of bean sprouts, 1 tablespoon chopped green onions, 1 tablespoon chopped bamboo shoots, 1 tablespoon finely chopped water chestnuts, 1 teaspoon Chinese flavoring powder. Salt to taste. Now add to this ¾ cup chopped seafood or cooked meat. Mix thoroughly. (Has there ever been a recipe that you

Egg Edibilities 103

didn't have to mix thoroughly?) Now put plenty of oil on a hot griddle or skillet and pour about ⅓ cup of egg mixture to form little cakes on same. Fry on a hot and fast fire. They will kind of swell up into thick cakes, but they won't blow up. Fry and keep turning until a delicate brown. Pile together for a serving and pour this sauce over them. *Sauce is:* 1 cup chicken broth, ¼ teaspoon sugar, little salt, 2 tablespoons soya sauce, 2 teaspoons Chinese flavoring powder, 1 tablespoon cold water. *Note:* Heat broth in a small pan, add rest of the stuff, and thicken as in gravy with cornstarch mixed in cold water. Don't ever say phooey to Foo Yong.

Ham ... and ... Eggs
(Think I'd forgotten????)

Ah, yes, the great American favorite, Ham and Eggs. But just a moment. *You've* et plenty of them—but *these*. Hey. They are *terrific ... tempting ... tantalizing ... tremendous ... and*

Tropical

I mean it. Listen, never in your life have you had anything like this, unless at one time or another you've had this. Take a look, a try, and I'll bet ten to one you'll repeat this plenty. Here:

Peel and split 1 banana for each person you are to serve. Fry them in butter. Set them aside to keep warm on a heated platter. Then in the same skillet fry slices of well-drained pineapple, 1 slice per serving. Put them aside for now, add more butter to the same skillet, and scramble or fry your eggs. The flavor is plumb out of this world. Never have you tasted such eggs. The ham is to be fried in a separate skillet. Now pile the eggs on one side of the plate, lay the pineapple and bananas on top of the ham on the plate. In another little saucepan make a thick syrup with brown sugar, butter, and a little water, and pour 1 tablespoon of said syrup over the bananas, pineapple, and ham. I have no comment at present, but when you try this you'll all have plenty to say.

Tomato Egg Basket

This dish is pretty and palatable and good eating as well as, I should imagine, good for you. The only thing I can think wrong with this, would be you had folks that didn't like tomatoes or eggs or both. But let's take a chance anyway:

At the stem side of large, ripe but fairly solid tomatoes, cut the stem mark out and carefully scoop out most of the pulp. Cut out enough to allow an egg to be poured in. Now sprinkle the inside of the scooped tomato with salt and pepper, adding celery or onion salt if 'n ya feel

Egg Edibilities

like it. Now break an egg in the tomato and cover the egg with the copped scoopings. Place the tomatoes in a pan, and place this pan in another partially filled with water. Then on top of each tomato place a piece of brown paper heavily spread with butter. Put in a moderate oven and bake. Should take about 30 minutes. If you want some bacon in the deal, remove the brown paper from the top for the last 10 or 15 minutes and put small bacon strips over the top. Eat with a fork, but have a spoon handy.

Double Boiler Omelet

Couple little tricks in this type, and cooked in a double boiler, the better to serve individual omelets:

For 4 omelets you use 8 eggs, ½ cup hot water, salt, a speck of cayenne for each omelet, 4 tablespoons of butter, and 1 tablespoon finely chopped chives. Now then, beat eggs well, adding seasoning and hot water. Cook in the aforementioned double boiler, stirring slowly and constantly until the mixture thickens like custard. Place a little butter in skillet and pour enough batter from boiler for 1 omelet (¼), same routine as always, and keep it up until all have been made and are quickly served on hot plates. Kinda tricky at that, by George.

Omelet Espaniole

'Twas a dark and stormy night, and a goodly crowd was there—
The folks was gettin' hungry—the hostess pulled her hair.
"I'm very tired, my cupboard's bare,
I haven't a scrap in the house to spare,"
She cried, and ranted, "What shall I do?"
    AUTHOR'S NOTE
Make a Spanish omelet—Don't let this happen to you.

This concoction is really a Spanish omelet deal, but it can be used on a number of leftover things. If you insist on using it on eggs, just make a plain omelet and shower it with this. But I repeat, this sauce can be used on a lot of things. Now for the sauce:

Put 6 tablespoons of butter in a frying pan, and when it's hot add 4 tablespoons of chopped onion, 4 tablespoons of chopped green pepper, 1 cup of peeled and chopped mushrooms, and 1 clove of garlic cut in half. Fry until a golden brown, then add a #2 size can of tomatoes. Season lightly with salt, pepper, and a speck of cayenne. Cook until thick, remove garlic, and serve on whatever you made it to serve on.

Super Egg Supper

Going to be a lotta putting in and taking out to arrive at the finale of this egg special, but if you've a moment or two to spare and like a good egg entree, take a crack at this:

Take a can (big) of whole packed tomatoes, a slice of bacon per head, 1 small onion, 1 pint of milk, grated Parmesan cheese, 3 tablespoons of butter, Worcestershire, salt and pepper. Prepare everything except the eggs you'll use later. Put the tomatoes and bacon in a pan and let them cook for 7 or 8 minutes. Take from oven and let stand till ya want them. Now cut the small onion up very fine and fry in a little butter until golden, then let stand. Now make some cream sauce. Butter some shirring dishes, break an egg in each, and place in hot oven. When about half cooked, remove and sprinkle some onion on each dish. Add one slice of bacon, halved, add tomato, and over all sprinkle a little Worcestershire. Pour some cream sauce over each dish and top with grated cheese. Put the dish under the broiling flame and brown cheese. You can try this in one big dish but it's tough to keep the eggs individual—however, it will work if you have calm nerves and a steady hand. Good luck to you.

THE EGGS ARE LAID

These honeys have become a personal triumph.

CHAPTER EIGHT

BAILEY'S BEST

Everyone has his favorite dishes. Through loving care these are honeys because they have been nursed, babied, paraded, bragged about, and have become a personal triumph. Most of the following I have never disclosed because I wanted to be selfish and the only living person who could run up batches like these. But in proof of my nuttiness I shall forthwith shoot the works on my special pride and joys. Through my tears I hurl at you the following:

Bailey's Iowa Baked Beans
(What a hit these have been for years)

Take a 2-pound bag of small navy beans and put them in a pot that will later hold the steam. Don't bother soaking them—do this: Cover them with cold water about an inch over them. Then add 2 or 3 heaping tablespoons of baking soda and bring this to a boil. Let it simmer a minute or so and then drain and rinse well. Put the pot back and fill it about ⅔ full of *boiling* water.

While the beans boil merrily along, chop fine 2 medium carrots and 1 good big onion. Add this to the boiling beans. Now here's a trick and one of the main secrets. Be sure you have bought (and paid for) 3 pounds of the finest pork available. It must be a high class cut of roast pork. Shoulder rib, but lay off that salt pork or ham. The better grade pork the better taste you'll get. Cut this up in hunks and shove it down in the porridge you have going on the stove. Salt and pepper the whole batch good, turn the fire down a little, and go read the paper for a couple hours till the beans are done. Don't let them get mushy and be sure the pork is *really* done. In case the water gets low and boils away (and believe me if you don't watch it, it will), add *boiling* water. Don't be afraid of getting this too soupy, but don't let it get mushy. When the beans are done you'll find all the carrots and onion pieces are nearly gone. Now stop right here. This is ready to serve this way if you want to have baked beans tomorrow. It's a wonderful main dish the way it is, but the folks that come to our house and also live here can't wait. They want the baked version *now* so this is what I do, and I modestly admit with great success.

The Baking of Beans á la Bailey

Take all the pork out and put it on a cutting board. Look carefully for little pieces of pork bones that might have cooked off the main hunk. Now you shred the pork

Bailey's Best

in very small pieces. Don't chop it, but go with the grain and pull it apart. When this is done, pour the beans and all the soup left into a baking crock. Now pay attention because here it comes. Add the pork to the beans. Take 4 heaping teaspoons of dry mustard and put in the middle. On top of this mustard put 5 or 6 heaping teaspoons of brown sugar, then pull out your bottle of Heinz 57 sauce and pour on about 6 *tablespoons* of same. Add some more salt and pepper and a quick dash or two of tabasco. Stir this thoroughly (don't smash the beans, take it easy but stir thoroughly). When this is all mixed, add at least a whole bottle of Heinz's tomato catsup. Be sure and use Heinz's as it is sweet and adds greatly to the flavor. After you've added the catsup, again mix thoroughly. In case they are still a little dry (they should be gooey) put a little water in the catsup bottle and add. Bake these in a medium oven for at least an hour or until a wonderful looking soft crust appears on the top. Serve with garlic (French) bread and cream cole slaw and you will be out of beans in no time at all. Writing this made me hungry for some and that's what I'm going to do right now. Have some?

Steako Supremo

If you follow this next just as I put it down, I can promise you a steak the like of which you've never had, unless you have been here at the house. If you have you'll know what I mean. If you try this steak you'll know what I mean. What I mean is try this steak.

Get a good pound of *top* sirloin, cut about 1¼ inches thick. (This serves two—add to it in exact proportions for more customers.) Put it on a cutting board and score it good. Score is a fancy name for whacking the dickens out of it with the sharp side of a butcher knife. Take some flour and knead it in the scored side, then whack it some more. Turn the steak over and do the same darn thing. While you're scoring the other side melt some suet in an iron skillet or any good *heavy* frying pan. Now the scores are even (ha ha) brown one side of it in the skillet. When brown, turn it over and start browning the other side. While its bottom side is being browned, take a lemon and squeeze the juice over the top side. Take a heaping teaspoon of dry mustard and with the spoon spread it around, making a paste. Then add 1 teaspoon of Worcestershire and again paste it up a little bit. Add salt and pepper and then cover this with Heinz's catsup—not too thick but paste it up again, adding a little more catsup if necessary. The oven should have been lit and not too hot by now, so you take the skillet and put it in the *top* shelf of the oven. Do not cover. Bake this little gem for about 20 minutes to half an hour or if you like real well done, use your own good judgment. You'll get scared the first time or two as the sauce and stuff turns kind of black, but inside, yipe. The reason you score it good and deep is to let the sauce and stuff seep down in. What a steak. I repeat, "What a steak."

Potato Salad Piperoo

Potato salad has been loved by a lot of old potato salad lovers. Honestly, mine isn't much different except a couple of little tricks to make it taste different, and usually the eater seems to enjoy the couple of little tricks I have conjured up.

Now start out like you always do by boiling an adequate number of potatoes in their skins. Let 'em cool (hey, don't boil them too soft!), then peel and cube them. After you have cubed them, put them in a bowl. Now remember what I said, don't cut them up too small because you are going to end up with a bowl that looks like mush.

Now look out for this one: Put some bacon in a frying pan, quite a little, and let her simmer, but when no one is looking, sneak over and get your bottle of cider vinegar and pour about 3 overflowing *teaspoons* of vinegar on the frying bacon. Be sure you do this real slow and watch it, or it will get away from you. When the bacon is crisp, put it on a paper towel to drain, but, for heaven's sake, save the grease and vinegar remaining in the pan because you will need that later.

Then dice your celery, a few sweet pickles, chop a big onion very fine, put them all on a plate ready to dump in when the time comes. If your folks like the taste of parsley, you can chop up a little of that, too.

Now, take a small mixing bowl and fill it up pretty good with a good type mayonnaise. Put in a dash of tabasco, Heinz 57 sauce, just a little tiny bit of chili sauce, enough cream or half and half. Now, stir this, kids, and stir it good. Take it gently over to the bowl of diced potatoes and pour it over the top, then carefully, with a wooden spoon and fork, mix. Don't *smash* the potatoes. Now let this stand a minute while you go over and reheat the grease and vinegar that is left in the skillet. When it is hot, pour this over the mixture of potatoes and dressing in the bowl and *carefully* mix again. Then break up your bacon very fine and spread all over the top, salt and pepper to taste, then mix again.

Now you see how I have tricked you into really getting this little beauty mixed. As I have learned and always say, you can't mix this kind of salad too well. But please, please, *please,* don't get it smashy and squishy.

Hamburger Sandwiches

Hamburger sandwiches, an old American favorite, can be glorified slightly by this sauce I stumbled on one day. Be sure you serve the hamburger on slightly toasted buns, if you can get them.

Fry the hamburgers like you always do, but before you do that, whip up this "stumbled sauce" I cracked about above. In a mixing dish, mix a fair amount of salad mayonnaise, equal part of chili sauce, 1 teaspoon vinegar and salad oil, dash of tabasco, dash of garlic salt, salt and pepper, and dash of cream. Then tear up a lot of lettuce and put it in until it is about solid—that is, the lettuce and the dressing. Kind of creamy, it should be, but if you are any good at this kind of stuff, at all, you will realize when she looks about ready. Put in the icebox and forget it.

Now fry your old hamburger steak or ground round, or you can grind some leftover beef and make into patties if you want to, and heat. Toast your buns, figure out something you would like to serve with this (but now you can see you won't need a salad), and put this cold sauce on the hot hamburgers just as you serve them. As the result of what people will say when they eat these hamburgers, please give me my credit.

P.S. I have never had a squawk on this sandwich for putting a piece of cheese on each hamburger, and let it melt a little bit just before you serve it. You're welcome.

Sweet Corn in the Husk

Being from Iowa, I am very fond of corn in any shape or form, but here is kind of a cute way of making corn on the cob a little different. Of course, you have got to do your own shopping, because you've got to get corn with full husks on. Now here's the recipe:

What you do first is take out all the silk but be careful and don't "bust a husk." Wash the corn good and then take a little piece of thin wire and pull the husk completely around the washed ear of corn. Then on the loose ends, wire them together. Then take some ice cubes and water in a pan and put each ear in the ice water, and if you have time (started your dinner on time), let the ears soak about ½ hour or more. When you are ready, get a grill and heat it. Place the ears on this grill and slowly cook. If I were you, I would watch these ears and turn them every so often. When the husks are sort of brownish all over, the corn is ready to eat. Now this is not baked or parched corn. It is perhaps the most luscious ear of sweet corn you have ever eaten. And that is all there is to it.

Ribs and Sauerkraut

You might enjoy a very easy and simple thing to do if you like ribs and sauerkraut. If you don't, you can save a lot of time and not even bother about reading the rest, because that is what it is.

You take some sauerkraut, canned (that is the easiest way out), and put it in a kettle that will have a tight-fitting lid later. Now you put this sauerkraut on top of the stove and finally, cut up very small a raw white potato. The reason for this is that it sweetens the sauerkraut. Now take another skillet or kettle and put your ribs in that without benefit of grease and start to lightly brown them. When the raw look is gone, slap them over into the sauerkraut and potato thing. Salt and pepper, a little bit more pepper, and let them simmer for a good hour. This I recommend especially for cold or rainy nights. It is savory, succulent, and usually successful.

Scalloped Stuffs

I claim no originality on this but I do think I have changed it around a little bit, and if you are told about it, it will serve as a reminder that someday you might thank me for. We like it at our house, and if you haven't tried it—try it!!

This same thing works with ham or pork chops plus macaroni *or* potatoes. Now that we are thoroughly confused, including me, let us see how this comes out. Supposing that you have some cold ham left, any kind, and you don't want to throw it away and you are tired of ham sandwiches or warmed over. Cube it right now, then boil some macaroni until it is about done, put the boiled macaroni under the water and wash it, then put the cubed ham in and salt and pepper, and some butter all through it, then slam it in the oven and let it bake. It shouldn't take long and it's pretty good.

Do the same thing with pork chops, but you better fry them first until they are almost done, then cube them.

Now if you want to do it with potatoes, why don't you prepare the potatoes like you were going to scallop them but thinner, the quicker for cooking, then do the same thing as above. I found with scalloped potatoes, that as you put each layer in, sift just a *little* flour over each layer, then add your meat, then your potatoes, which is harder than the macaroni, because with the macaroni, you just stir it up and if you are going to scallop the potatoes, you got to put them in by layers.

I am sure you know, but if you don't, you know you are supposed to cover each dish with a quantity of milk. Now if you like stuff like this gooey, put in a lot of milk. If you don't, naturally don't put in so much. If you want to make either of these dishes and want to make them better, put in a little good American cheese.

Bailey's Best

Bailey's Swiss Steak

Swiss steak is a memorable and ever-lovin' way of making hungry folks happy. You have your way—here is mine:

Take a good piece or two of round steak and quarter it. You don't have to measure to an exact quarter, but what I mean is, cut it in servable hunks (if you have heard this, stop me, but in case you don't know, be sure and cut all steaks cross grain—if you don't, it will make the meat tough on both you as a cook and the poor guy that has to chew it!). Now brown this in suet and use a kettle that goes on top of the stove. Brown this thoroughly. After it is brown, salt and pepper well, then pour over same a small can of tomato paste. Now let this meat and tomato paste bubble and giggle at you while you prepare several other little things.

Take a very small mixing crock (whatever that is) and take about 2 tablespoons of flour and add at least 2 cups of hot water. Now stir this good until it is completely de-lumped. Add a little more salt and pepper, a shot of tabasco, dash of cooking sherry, a spot of Heinz 57, and then stir it up good.* Add this gravy-type mix-

---

* I have always wanted to use one of these asterisks, which means either the editor or me, or both, forgot something, which I just did. What I wanted to tell you was this. In any gravy, including the one you are making above, if you boil potatoes, save the water you boil them in and instead of using plain-unpotatoed water, use the potato water with the flour, and, by golly, it makes a difference. Now where were we . . . oh, yes, back to the recipe. Please refer above.

ture to the bubbling and giggling steak and tomato sauce. Then, not slice, not mince, not chop, not cube, but *quarter* a good-sized onion, and after you have mixed the goober well, gently drop the quartered onion over the top so that the steam will come up, the juice will go down through the gunk in the pot. Turn the fire low as soon as it is all simmering away merrily and go read the paper or play gin rummy with the hubby for at least 1½ hours. Of course, it won't hurt to peek in the pot and turn the meat over and kind of help things along. Comments on this recipe have been "Hmm!" This tastes like some Old World recipe. But, as you can see, it isn't. It is just an old American idea. Hope you like it. I thank you.

Spanish Bean Pot

This recipe, if you are going to make it, must be made by a person with strong nerves and a belief in me, because it is what we in the show business call a real production. Incidentally, the recipe that I am about to unfurl will serve at least ten people. As a matter of fact, I have stretched it to fifteen people. Three, I am sure, were not hungry. However, this recipe, if you enjoy it at all, is like eating popcorn . . . the more you eat, the more you want, which may run you a little short at the end of the dinner. Good luck.

Bailey's Best

Six cans of a good brand of kidney beans. I use the bottom of a big roaster for this whole deal and you had better, too, because you don't have to cover it. After you read what's coming, you can see as well as I can it will probably blow up! Now add the following and with each addition, stir well into the beans. Four teaspoons of dry mustard, 2 teaspoons powdered cloves, look out now, *do not* put in over ½ *teaspoon* of cayenne pepper (you are stirring this all the time, aren't you?), 2 cups pineapple juice, 8 tablespoons of bacon grease, 4 tablespoons of cider vinegar. Now stir this around extra-special, then leave it alone for a minute. Go over to the chopping block and chop 3 small onions, just chop them up regular like. They don't have to be too fine. As soon as your eyes are dry, put the onions in with the stuff you already have in the bean pot. Now add at least 2 teaspoons of salt. Cook this whole thing in the oven about 1½ hours and stir it real often.

Do this after about 1½ hours: add a cup of black coffee. If you haven't got any left from breakfast, cook some. Liquid coffee, that is . . . no coffee grounds! Then add 3 ounces of cooking brandy. Lay about ½ pound of bacon strips across the top, put it back in the oven, and cook until the bacon is crisp. My suggestion again is serve French bread with a little garlic salt and butter between each slice, and a creamy cabbage coleslaw. For dessert—they will probably want some more of these beans.

Mrs. B's Icebox Freeze
(but don't really freeze it)

Here is a Bailey's Best, but if you want me to be honest, it isn't Jack Bailey's Best, it is Carol Bailey's Best (that is my wife by marriage). Now, Mrs. Bailey is a little worried because she cooks like I do, hoping it comes out right, so if this icebox dessert doesn't come out, please contact *Mrs.* Bailey, not me!!

Mrs. Bailey says, "I think I've got this right. I'm not sure, but here is the way I do it. Cream in a large mixing bowl 1 cup of sugar and about 1 tablespoon butter and add yolk of an egg (beat the white separately to be added later). Now, wait a minute, let me think. Use 1 can crushed pineapple (or chop canned pineapple), about ½ cup chopped walnuts, 6 to 8 cut marshmallows*. Add stiffly beaten egg white. Take 12 to 16 graham crackers, ground fine with a rolling pin, line a china or glass serving plate with these crumbs, pour the above mixture over the crumbs, adding remaining cracker crumbs on the top, and put in the icebox to harden. Allow this to thicken in the icebox several hours. Serve in squares, topping with whipped cream."

---

* May I tell you gals a trick that Mrs. Bailey uses. In cutting marshmallows, take some common ordinary sewing shears, dip in water, clip a marshmallow, dip again in water, and clip away. Excuse me, Carol, for butting in.

Meat Pie—The Easy Way

All of us get lazy and tired of cooking but still we try to please the receivers of our vittles. Even if it is sometimes practically effortless. So here is a bunch of stuff in one pot and if you've got a fairly good can opener, a little time and a sense of blending, you will find yourself a bit of a success. It is a homemade meat pie which can hardly come out wrong. Here we go.

Get 1 pound of chuck, cut it into fairly small hunks. Put about 2 cups of water over this and let it simmer for a good hour. As soon as that is over, put it in a baking dish, keeping it warm all the time.

Now open a can of peas and pour the peas and the juice over this stewing meat. Chop fine 3 to 4 fresh carrots, chop up about 4 stalks of celery, and a few celery leaves—about ½ cup. Open a #2 can of spinach and use about half and all the juice. What you are going to do with the remaining half of the dry spinach is your worry. Add also 1 very small onion chopped fairly fine. Take about 4 medium potatoes, peel and quarter them, put them in another pan, add some cream and a little water, and slowly boil them until they have boiled down to a creamy consistency. Now your potatoes are set, the other stuff is set, the beef, I hope, is done by now and has simmered through this other stuff, so add salt and pepper, tabasco sauce if you desire (just a squirt), also a slight squirt of Heinz 57, then stir this up well. Now spread the potatoes over the top and *don't* stir again. Put this in a medium oven and let it go.

Then, if you are clever and lucky enough, make a pie crust, or if you wait like I do, make one of those prepared pie crusts out of a box, add a little water, roll it out, and put it over the top of this. When the crust is brown, take 'er out, call the folks, and go to it.

Homemade Chili Con Carne

Lots of people are very fond of chili; it can be used in so many ways, like over spaghetti, over macaroni, over hamburgers, or leftover meat, but so many people are afraid to try to make it at home. Don't be. Take a look at this, try it, and you'll like it. That is, of course, if you like chili. Here's the recipe:

First thing you'd better do is chop up 3 or 4 medium onions and simmer same in a little fat with 1 large green pepper until the whole mess is tender. Add to the onion and pepper 1 pound of ground steak and brown this all nicely. Before you start this whole thing, sneak down to the grocery store, buy—and pay for—1 can of good grade chili, 1 can of red beans. Now, of course, we know you've got that so you add that to the above. Then put in 1 cup of tomato juice *or* a can of tomato soup *or* a can of tomato sauce, then dump in about ¼ teaspoon of curry powder. Add salt and pepper, and as much chili powder as you feel you and the folks can stand. Look out for that chili powder! It's really tough if you get too much. Stir this up good, cover, and let it cook in a slow oven for a couple of hours.

The dropper-inners.

CHAPTER NINE

QUICKIES!

Quickies Introduction

Shudders, horrors, screams, and fainting spells have been caused due to unexpected dropper-inners. The following chapter is dedicated to those thousands. Now "Quickies" don't mean they are quick to cook—but usually quick to prepare, then go to the front room and glare—but something will come out pretty well and without too much trouble. If you glance carefully through this Quickie chapter you'll find a good many recipes that call for things on hand, so best check them and as the Scouts say, and it applies to cooks also, "Be Prepared."

Spanish Rice

Right off the bat excuse yourself and go soak one cup of rice. Pull down a pot or kettle of Club Aluminum, Silver Seal, or some such vessel that will later keep the steam in when covered. Put some grease or drippings in bottom of same and brown thunder out of 1 cup of chopped onions and 1 cup of chopped celery—together. The aroma of this will filter into the other room and the folks will start getting hungry—but you tell them to be quiet and add 1 pound of ground round or a reasonable facsimile, stir and mess this around with the above and then put in a big (I mean big!) can of tomatoes. Mess this up some too as you add a couple of tablespoons of Worcestershire and best add salt and pepper to taste. *Now quit stirring. Please!* Remember the rice you've been soaking all this time? Sprinkle it *lightly* on top of stuff you have been working on, cover tightly, and let 'er steam from 30 to 45 minutes. Don't stir again, and don't get scared when it bubbles up and looks awful. She's okay in this same old way.

Tricky Tuna

Here's a Cutie Quickie that's a dandy. When you read and learn how simple it is, eat it and find out how good it is, you'll just love me forever for telling you:

All you need is a sack of potato chips, a can of good tuna, a can of mushroom soup, and some milk or half and half. Take a glass baking dish, put a light layer of potato chips on bottom, layer of tuna on that, layer of potato chips on that, layer of tuna on that, layer of potato chips on that. Keep up that same layer routine till the dish is full or you are out of stuff. Then over the top pour the can of mushroom soup, and the same can full of milk or half and half. Bake this in a medium oven until it sorta gravies up, and it shouldn't take very long. If it takes longer than you want it to, just turn the oven up a little.

Late Returner's Ragout

Listen, Ladies—Important!—if you play bridge too long, shop too long, fiddle around all afternoon and you've got to feed the folks soon, here's a pip of a one-dish-meal that's wonderful. You'll be a hit with the family and can stay out again some afternoon.

Take one of those pots that keep the steam in and put 1 layer of bacon in the bottom. (Canadian is fine but so is the regular.) Get some round steak, about a pound and a half, and cut in inch strips. I hope you know that if you cut it cross grain it will be more tender. Put 1 or 2 layers of this on top of the bacon, sprinkle some black pepper on this (whole pepper helps), then put the lid on the pot and turn the flame very low. Next you take about 5 or 6 carrots and slice them penny-wise about ¼ inch thick. Lay them flat in about two layers over the round steak. (This whole meal comes out in sections.) Then take a couple of big onions and slice them as thin as you can (we all have eye trouble doing this but it's worth it). Put these thin slices flatly on the carrots. Then peel about five potatoes and use one of those mechanical slicers so the potatoes are paper thin, and of course that will make about an inch layer of thin sliced potatoes on top. I almost forgot to tell you to salt and pepper lightly over each layer. There's your pot full, now take a cup of cold water and gently pour over the whole batch. Cover tightly and let it go for about 40 minutes still over a low flame. During the 40 minutes you can make salad, dessert, and think of some excuse why you were out all day and what excuse you can use next time.

Casserole Noodling

Speaking of Quickies, and we still are, take a try at this little dilly. On all occasions it's termed Yummy.

Grab yourself 2 pounds of veal and make enough broth with it to get 6 cups of veal broth. (Naturally it must be veal to get the veal broth.) Now girls, you can use 6 cups of canned consommé if you're dropped in on, but it honestly isn't as good. So in the 6 cups of veal broth you boil a 6-ounce package of fine noodles. The liquid will almost disappear, but don't worry—it should. Drag down your favorite casserole dish and start putting stuff in by layers. Alternate starting with the noodles, then a layer of hard-boiled eggs (2) sliced of course . . . 3 tablespoons minced green pepper . . . ½ cup of sliced stuffed olives . . . ¼ cup of mushrooms chopped and sautéed in butter. Be sure and finish with layer of noodles. Grate cheese over the top and brown the whole thing in the oven. Oughta take ya about 20 minutes.

Wienie Bake

The preparation and baking of this should be done in less than an hour—resulting in a combo that is a cinch to please everyone. The Wienie Bake in this manner will make no one groan as a result of the eating of hot dogs—baking beats boiling in this case, it makes you feel better as well as making it taste better. Now quick like a flash do this:

Take a low buttered casserole, slice 2 medium onions, and make a layer in the bottom, then a layer of a sliced green pepper. Next, quarter about 4 medium tomatoes (or 1 large can of whole tomatoes), salt and pepper, and then pour in 1 can of *niblet* corn. Top this with a pound of wienies (garlic type if possible) and bake for about 40 minutes. Now, the first time I tried this I baked it too fast, so be sure the oven isn't too hot, bring it all up together in a medium oven. And bring all the eaters up together and see how quick a Quickie can disappear.

Beef Hunk Humdinger

Here we may proceed with either leftovers or fresh meat. The leftovers make the Quickie quicker, but the fresh start makes the flavor a bit better. Sauté 1½ pounds of round steak in 1½ inch cubes. When they are good and brown put them in the bottom of a pot with a tight lid. Then add 1 #2 can of tomatoes and 1 #1 can of niblet corn, ½ teaspoon of basil, a pinch of nutmeg, salt and pepper. Let this go for about ½ hour and serve. If you use leftovers skip the sauté, and just cook long enough to thoroughly heat and blend. Serve some light brown bread or make some corn bread, slap some lettuce and dressing around some place, and go to it. There's quite a Quickie and we use it often.

Celery and a Stewed Ham Hunk

That's not a very good name for this, because it's misleading. I first was exposed to this at the home of my former secretary. After the way I ate, long and lusty, she quit secretarying and got married as a result of my eating and bragging to her sweetie about her cooking. I found out later how easy it was to make, so it made me a liar about her great cook-stove talents, but it's a good dish even if the name isn't. Now what did she say to do first, oh yesss:

Cut up a couple of bunches of celery and steam a little while with a little water in a pot with a tight lid. Steam about 5 or 10 minutes and then add some diced baked ham (if you use fresh or raw ham start it with the celery, but if not, add the cooked ham to the celery) and steam together about 6 or 7 minutes more. Make a rather thick cream sauce, then drain the celery and ham as well as possible, and pour over it the cream sauce. Add a little dry mustard, stir in a bit of dry basil, and let stew until it feels done, but not too thick or hardened. Get one of those prepared muffin recipes and make a fruit muffin or two, then serve a vegetable salad of some nice light nature, and if you are the fancy type, pour the stewed stuff over some very thin melba toast. Hit it with a bit of paprika over the top, and go join the natives as they eat and enjoy this celery and stewed ham hunk. You'll *not* be sorry!!!

Tuna Casserole-Like

So this will take an hour, but what's an hour in a busy life. Right! An hour. However, friends, this hour is well spent, and you won't have to spend it over the stove. This is not a fish dish, but a good supply of eatin'. Best have the trusty can opener around again as this is all from cans. A man or woman cook can't go wrong on this, and neither can you, whoever you are. Do it like this:

First, find the egg beater. When found, find 2 eggs. Now all found, beat the 2 eggs with the beater but good. Now add to this 1 large can of evaporated milk, a good-sized can of creamed corn, and a regular size can of flaked tuna. Grate a medium onion and chop a medium green pepper and add both of these. Mix well, put in a buttered glass baking dish or casserole, and bake medium like for about an hour. How does that sound? Good? You're right. It is.

Spinach Bacon Noodle-Doodle

Now here we have a bit of ovening that's worth the gas it will take. So you have an electric stove, it's still worth the juice:

Cook a package of fine noodles in boiling salted water till tender. Drain a can of spinach and cover noodles that you should have placed in the bottom of a baking dish. Season well with salt, pepper, butter, and quite a slug of grated onion. Forgot to tell ya that while above is going on crisp up several pieces of bacon and drain on a paper towel; if this all comes out even, lay bacon over above mixture and cover with about 2 cups of cream sauce. Sprinkle bread crumbs, dot with butter, n' then cover thickly with grated cheese. Bake this until well heated and well browned. No potatoes—no trouble, just salad and this makes a meal, not counting dessert. That's up to you. But a Noodle-Doodle is a dandy-doodle not to be ignored. Please, I implore—*don't ignore!!!!!*

The Ball of the Corned Beef

I have always worried about the cooking and serving of corned beef from scratch. Well, sir, I found that they have corned beef in cans, which saves the interminable toil of going through the whole process. Here is a quicklike get-up that can be served at the drop of a ball in deep fat, and it's something that tasted so good I couldn't leave it out. I had it and couldn't believe it could taste that good after watching the way it was done:

Take a can of corned beef and grind the very divvil out of it. Now mix in a raw egg and mix good. Then shape into balls around an olive with an onion center, or just a small pickled onion. Make a fairly thick cream sauce and after the corned beef balls have been rolled in dried bread crumbs and dropped in deep fat until thoroughly heated, pour this cream sauce over them and serve on melba or plain toast. A wee bit of salad (fruit type), some cranberry sauce or a tart jelly, and you've got yourself a quick-flick of a meal. I'm sure it's a better lunch than dinner, but you might even try it for breakfast. Wait a minute! How about trying this for a midnight snack? Hmmmm. If I could stay awake that long some night I might.

Meat and Potato Cake

Quick like a wind, a wink, a whisper, a whistle. Put this together and believe me, this'll—be mighty welcome in a hurry. All you'll need is stuff you've got on hand, and for some silly reason it tastes like something you've planned. This fits for breakfast through lunch, through dinner, through the time your guests of the evening have stayed late and gotten hungry. Versatile is the usage of this particular conglomeration:

In a lightly greased skillet, grate a potato per person. Then search the icebox for leftover ham, corned beef, beef, pork, or fresh bacon. Whatever the search discloses, chop it up very fine and mix with the grated potatoes. Grate just a small hunk of fresh onion (enough only to flavor), and then the usual salt and pepper to taste. Press in one cake or individual cakes, and brown on each side until potatoes are done. If you use bacon, it will take a shade longer, natch. From then on it's up to you to think of things like slamming a poached egg on each cake, whipping up some toast with a spread, jumbling up a salad, or just letting it go as it is. And as it is, it is good. It is, it is.

Rare Welsh Rarebit

This is good anytime, welcome anytime, and anytime you want it, do this anytime. It's worked for me most anytime so now is the time to tell you about it, so anytime you want it you'll have it:

Make up 2 cups of cream sauce by blending 2 tablespoons of butter, 2 tablespoons of flour, and 2 cups of milk. Add 3 cups of freshly grated cheese (nippy), ¼ teaspoon of cayenne, and 4 teaspoons of dry mustard. Now blend and reblend until it's smooth and creamy. Flavor this whole business with 4 tablespoons of cooking sherry and serve in a bowl or chafing dish with crisp buttered melba toast on the side. This is grand for late dropper-inners, lunch dropper-inners, or even *without* dropper-inners .

No canapé at Waikiki!

CHAPTER TEN

CANAPÉS
CANOPYS
HORS D'OEUVRES
(French for tidbits)

> *You'll see Mrs. B and me*
> *Far across the sea*
> *Not worrying about a canapé*
> *On the Beach of Waikiki.*

So many alleged hosts or hostesses decide that it's too much trouble to fuss around with little junky things before a meal when entertaining. Now that is a downright shame. It just takes a few minutes and marks you as a smart entertainer when you dash out with some loaded plates of cute canapés. Now look over this chapter and be advised that it's worth not only looking over but worth doing. Most folks just serve stale popcorn and peanuts. Don't do it. Do some of these. Please.

Sardine-Stuffed Bacon

Smash up a can of good sardines and slip in a little Worcestershire, a few specks of dry mustard, and a dash of pepper. Spread this combo on some bacon pieces, roll 'em up, fasten with a toothpick, and sauté until the bacon is crisp. Leave the toothpicks in and they can use them for handles to eat with.

Cheese-Bacon-Blitz

Slap an egg yolk until it's really beat, then add about $\frac{1}{2}$ cup of grated nippy cheese, around about a tablespoon of cream, and some salt and pepper. Toast some bread squares or rounds and spread this mixture on the untoasted side. Whack up some bacon in about 1 inch pieces and put on the top of this. Toast in an oven until the bacon is good and crisp. You try . . . you like!

(So far so good, eh? Please turn to next page.)

Bacon Avocado Smash

Get this one. Make a mushy spread of avocado smashed and seasoned with a little salt, a dash of paprika, and a slight squirt of fresh lemon juice. Spread on toast strips and sprinkle with chopped bacon. *Broil* until crisp.

Miniature Meat Pies

This and the following you can use for a lot more than just canapé purposes. Teas, lunches, with soup, snacks, and suppers. Take two egg yokels, ½ cup of regular butter, 2 tablespoons of cream (or half and half), 2 cups of flour, and pinch in a little salt. Mix into a dough and then roll it out very, very, very thin and cut in circles with the usual cookie cutter or an old clean tin can. Now grind yourself some leftover cooked meat and add just a swish of grated onion. Season a bit and add some leftover gravy to moisten. No gravy? A dot of butter, then. Put on circles, fold over and bake in an oven of about 350°. Wonderfully wonderful.

Sneak Meat Rolls

This is so quick and fine and easy you'll be glad I thought to tell you about it. Get some nice fresh liverwurst sausage. Make some dough out of any of those boxed biscuit deals. Put the liverwurst on it, roll it, slice it, bake it, eat it. You'll love it.

Liver in an Egg

How tired most people seem to be of the usual corny-type stuffed eggs. Take a bit of time out after you have boiled some eggs and mix this up. Halve eggs lengthwise and remove yolks. Mix with some liverwurst and mash this good. Put in some salt, add a bit of cayenne, dry mustard, Worcestershire, lemon juice, and mayonnaise. Heap this in the whites and chill. If you are late don't chill. Don't spill. Just serve and be praised.

Cucumber Cutie

This, my friends, is a sang-wich that really sings. Boy, it's good. Just take and peel a cuke and remove the center and the seeds. Best do this with an apple corer (if you have one). Now mix 1 package of cream cheese, 2 tablespoons of chopped chives, 2 teaspoons of chopped parsley, ¼ teaspoon of mustard, and enough mayonnaise to soften. Stuff the de-seeded and de-centered cucumber with this, then gently wrap in waxed paper and place in the refrigerator. When nice and cool and firm, slice thin and serve on some rounds of rye bread toasted and well buttered. Now, if I may coin a phrase, I will . . . "Ya got somethin' there." And you have.

Canapés, Canopys, Hors D'Oeuvres

Celery Stuffin'

In thinking of stuffing a celery stalk or two for parties and dinners everyone (mostly) mutters Roquefort cheese and paprika. Now a Roquefort mess is coming up next, but for a different stuffin' with celery use this.

Mash up some liverwurst and add some lemon juice to taste and chopped-up stuffed green olives. Now thin this out a bit with a nice, creamy mayonnaise. (One of the biggest secrets of stuffed celery is to use the small inside stalks with this secret stuffin'.)

Roquefortish Smear

So you won't be happy until there's a slight smash of Roquefort around the premises. Okay. To keep you happy and the eaters happy and everybody happy (if they and you like Roquefort) smear up this smear in this manner.

Mix ½ pound of butter and ½ pound of Roquefort cheese. Mix it good and then dump in a couple cakes of cream cheese and smear this all together. Now add a little minced parsley, a spoon of anchovy paste, just a slight squirt of lemon juice, and a dash of paprika. Let this chill all night and when you want to use it throw in a little cream until it looks about right. Put it in a cute bowl, surround it with cute crackers. There you have a smear.

Coleslawed Ham Slaw

Here's a fooler. This you can use for a sandwich spread, an hors d'oeuvre spread, or most any kind of spread. The reason I mentioned fooler is the fact no one would ever think this combination would turn out so good, but it does when the performance goes like this:

Get a solid head of cabbage and a sharp knife. Cut your head in two and take out your heart. Then shred very, very thin. After shredding your head very, very thin, mince it very, very mincey. So much for your little head right now. At this point you run some cooked ham scraps or sliced boiled ham through a chopper and add to the cabbage with some mayonnaise. Then flavor it with a lot of lemon juice. A little celery seed and dry mustard and mix it up good and mixed. Don't be fooled and not use this fooler.

Stuffed Sliced Square Rolls

Now start this one early as it has to chill. Preparation is easy and quick and you can go on about your other chores with time to spare.

Canapés, Canopys, Hors D'Oeuvres 145

Now we'll mix about 3 packages of Philadelphia cream cheese with a couple tablespoons of butter and 3 tablespoons of chopped chives. Little Worcestershire, paprika, and salt. Now we'll hollow out the centers of square French rolls and fill with the above, and then place in the refrigerator for at least 4 hours. After that and when you are good and ready, simply slice and serve the stuffed sliced square rolls. Ain't that slick?

Creamed White and Green

So many people rave about this canapé that it's almost a must at our house. It's passed so many pleasant polls that I'm sure it will get *your* vote too. This is the Bailey way, but if something shows up hereunder you'd like to leave out, it wouldn't be too serious. Here's what I do:

Cream thoroughly 4 tablespoons of butter and 2 packages of cream cheese. When she's good and smooth add a little salt, a teaspoon of capers, a slight spoon of paprika, 2 or 3 finely chopped green onions (both top and bottoms), and 2 finely chopped anchovies. Stir this around good and put to one side in a cool place. Just before you serve it, toast some thin bread and place in top of oven to melba, then spread this stuff on the toast and serve. It's as good as it is pretty and I wish you the success we've had with this.

Sticks of Cheese

Billions of potato chips, bread sticks, and crackers are used with canapés. Why not whip up a homemade and unusual thing that will surprise everyone and then you'll be different from the billions of people who serve potato chips, bread sticks, and crackers.

Simply mix a cup of flour, ½ teaspoon of salt, and a cup of freshly grated cheese with 2 heaping tablespoons of butter. Mix very well, roll out, cut in long strips, and bake in a medium oven until done. That will make you one in a billion.

Don't be fooled—there are no carrot recipes here.

CHAPTER ELEVEN

VEGETABLES

Vegetables

When people think of vegetables they usually think, well I'll have some carrots, some peas, some . . . - - - . . . oh, anything I can use a can opener to. Ya know! Why not put a little thought and time on the poor old vegetable end of a meal, and with it you will have a well-rounded meal. The swell part of vegetables in cooking is the fact that while the main dishes are cooking you have plenty of time to get a shade fancy, add a little something, and have not just a vegetable but another fancy dish. Carry on from here if you think I'm right.

Corn

I've made a living of talking corn, I like to eat corn, and I have some more corn (cooked this is) I'd like to talk about. Let me tell you of a trick way to make some corn.

Open a #2 can of creamed corn. Pour in a bowl and then salt and pepper well. Add about 1½ cups of milk, and break up a dozen or so soda crackers in it. Stir this fairly well and when mixed, put a large hunk of butter in the center and on top, so it will melt and spread during the cooking. Break up in large pieces about 3 or more crackers and put them on top as little posts and then shove in the oven. When the posts are browned and the corn is boiling, it's done. The corn on top gets brown, and it is really a dish worth trying to serve with chicken, beef, pork, lamb, hamburger, veal, and . . . - - - most anything. Good.

Spinach Ahhhhhhhhhhhhhhhhh

When spinach is mentioned don't let anyone go BLAHHHHHHHHH! Got one here that takes the curse off spinach, because it's not as bad as everyone says. Take a listen to this, and it's so good I can even eat it. I didn't used to like spinach, but this way I do.

Par-fry (new term) some bacon, about 2 strips. Don't fool with fresh spinach; open a can and pour in a baking dish, juice and all with the par-fried bacon. Shoot a shot of tabasco, a little Lea and Perrins, a broken egg, some crumbled fresh crackers, and mix this well. After you have mixed this, smooth it out and place strips of American cheese over the top. Put this in—when it comes out,

Vegetables 151

it will not taste like the ordinary spinach. They'll say Ahhhhhhhhhhh!

Rice Chinatown

This is the famous Chinese fried rice and a mighty popular dish with lovers (of rice). If you run out of potato ideas and want a swell change in your menu, best take a careful glance at the as follows:

The rice you are to use must be cooked a long time before using. It's better if you have rice cooked the day before you use it. Now to start with fried rice, take a couple tablespoons of peanut oil or good fresh cooking oil and add ½ cup of finely diced ham, chicken, or pork (cooked). Fry this lightly and add about 3 finely sliced mushrooms, 1 green onion finely chopped, 2 tablespoons of soya sauce, and 1 quart of cold cooked rice. Continue to fry for about 10 minutes. Fry 'er slow tho'. Now, beat up an egg real well, add to frying mixture, and continue for another 5 minutes. If you want the color a little deeper add a bit more of soya sauce. Now that, my friends, is honest-to-goodness fried rice, and it's as good as it sounds.

French Fried Bailey—Onions

What a hit this is, and what a simple procedure. With steak or roast they add just the right touch and are easier to make than you'd think.

Like for instance, you cut in rings several good fresh sweet onions, and soak them in cold milk for about 15 minutes or so. Then get some deep fat jumping hot, and when the fat is ready, put the milk-soaked onions in some flour until they are covered well, and drop in the deep fat. That's all, but when they are nice and brown take them out and drain on wax paper, or I just use paper towels. Now you know, let's see ya go.

Cabbage Common

So many folks say "Yipe" at the thought of cabbage. They always think immediately of indigestion, but that is not the fault of the dear old cabbage—it's the fault of the cooking method. Do it this way, and you'll see. (This also applies to broccoli and brussels sprouts.) Doesn't even smell up the house when cooked this way.

Start the whole thing off with two pots of boiling water. No covers on the pots. While they are coming to a boil, wash, cut, and quarter a nice big head of cab-

Vegetables 153

bage. Take stalk right out, leaving the leaves free. Now put this in a bowl of cold water. In one of the boiling pots put a teaspoon of baking soda and the cabbage—let it boil not a second longer than 3 minutes, strain water off, and refill the pot with the fresh boiling water from the other pot. Let this boil until cabbage is tender, then drain and cut up cabbage. Do not add grease or butter to cabbage, but serve exactly as it is—it will be fragrant, fresh, and digestible. Not only that, it will be good to eat, too.

Mickey Fine Vegetables

Vegetable combinations always end up as carrots and peas mixed. They have the usual dull and ordinary taste, so let's monkey around with this combination and fool the eaters, eh?

Cook separately some green peas, string beans (cut diagonally), and small pieces of potato balls and a little salt pork, also some baby lima beans. When cooked, drain and place all of them in a double boiler that has some melted butter in it. Add quite a few finely chopped bits of parsley and gently mix the vegetables while they are blending. How about that concoction for a vegetable to serve with anything?

Zucchini Corn Puddin'

Here is a fooler. This daisy dish is one to remember, and when you make it the people that eat it won't let you forget it. It goes like so:

Cook 6 large zucchini in boiling salted water until tender. Chop them up and drain them. Now, finely chop 2 onions, a clove of garlic, and a bell pepper. Sauté these chopped little fellows in butter, then cool and mix them with the zucchini. Add ½ cup of grated cheese, 5 well-beaten eggs, and a can of small kernel corn. Stir in ¼ cup of butter and pour into a baking dish. Place in a pan of hot water and bake in a slow oven for about an hour. Good folks like good food so there's a dish that is good.

Cauliflower Ear Special

Suppose we take a little cauliflower, a little cheese (Parmesan), and whip up a natural dish that some eaters might turn up their nose at—but not this one, and I'll tell you why. Here!!!

Boil the cauliflower whole in salted water until tender—drain and put in a large baking dish. Now take 2 tablespoons of evaporated milk and put in the top of a double boiler. Add ¼ pound grated cheese (Parmesan), 2 tablespoons Worcestershire sauce, 1 teaspoon lemon juice, and a pinch of nutmeg, pepper, and salt. Stir it slow over hot water (without boiling) until the sauce is thicklike. Spread it over the cauliflower and sprinkle on a lot of bread crumbs and grated cheese. Slap in the oven and brown this and then serve it. Right fittin' vittles, for right fittin' vittles.

Beets that Beat Beets

Here's a bit of beet cooking that makes a special flavor. You just do this as directed and even you, knowing what's happened to the beets, will hardly recognize the good old-fashioned beet.

Drain 1 can of small beets and save the juice. Now melt 2 tablespoons of butter and add 2 tablespoons of sugar—mix with 1½ tablespoons of flour. Add a couple tablespoons of lemon juice and gradually add ½ cup of the beet juice. Let cook until thickened. Now heat the beets in double boiler and pour into a casserole. Add 1 cup of hot cream to the beet juice mixture and pour over beets. Cover thickly with ground nut meats and brown lightly under your broiler. Ain't that somethin'? Wait till ya try it.

Spinach—Lettuce á la Wilted

Most all the folks I know like this wilted spinach or lettuce. If you are going to use lettuce be sure you get the good old Midwest leaf lettuce. Any leaf spinach will do. But you have got to fuss a bit with this. However, when it comes up with a meal you'll be glad. 'Specially good with a beef meal or maybe one with pork. Take a whack at it and see if I'm not right. Goes like this:

Wash good and proper ½ pound of leaf lettuce or spinach leaves, and let them stand in a bowl of ice water for at least a half hour. Lift them from their ice bath and drain, dry, and de-ice on a towel. Shred the leaves in a salad bowl and then add 1 small grated onion, 4 or 5 slices of fried bacon, the crisper the better, break over leaves, and then chop up the white of 1 hard-boiled egg. Season with salt, pepper, and a dash of cayenne. Mix this up very well with forks and tossing style. Now take ⅓ cup of cider vinegar, smash the yolk of the boiled egg, and add to the bacon fat. Let this come to a boil and pour over whichever green leaves you are using. Better do this just as the entree is coming to a head—'cause it won't be good if it stands after the hot stuff is poured over it. This should (and will) serve about 5 people.

Author's Note: I like it much better with leaf lettuce than spinach. I do know a thieving soul, however, that has done the same thing with turnip greens. That I've never tried, and if you do it, it's at your own risk. Thanx.

A head of lettuce.

CHAPTER TWELVE

SALUDAS TO SALADS (Si)

Salads—they can make or break a meal, not to mention a cook's rep. I find that these big production salads with nine thousand different condiments are a little unnecessary. Simple salads seem so sure, sweet, and swell. Thus I put them first. However, for you show-offs there will be a couple of trick ones. Okay? Okay!

Pear and Cheese

This is easy, sure-fire, and not too many people know about it.

Make a nest of lettuce on salad plate (individual). Put 2 canned half pears on top of same—slap a bit of mayonnaise lumped on pears, then grate thinly, but in long strands, some cheddar (smoky) cheese on top. You may use any cheese you like. Put in icebox to chill and serve when ready. This is really a good deal, and especially fine when the main course is a bit heavy.

Peach and Cottage Cheese

I should be ashamed, perhaps, for jotting this down as most of you know it—but maybe it will stumble its way to someone that doesn't.

Crisp outer leaves of head lettuce, bowl shape on individual plate. Two canned half peaches on top, mound of cottage cheese, pinch of sugar, drop of mayonnaise (if desired), and red cherry on top. That's all, folks.

Old-Fashioned Sweet Slaw

This is one of my favorite quickies. Easy, but high edibility.

Cut cabbage in half and slice thin but clear across the face and put in bowl. Now take a small bowl and throw in a cup of cream (half and half or canned). Add vinegar to taste and to thicken a bit. Then a little sugar. Just fuss around with this till it tastes like you want it to taste, and pour over cabbage and mix just before serving.

Avocado Smash

This I learned in old Mexico. With certain people, with certain things, and at certain times it's perfect. Some like—some don't. Good luck on your timing.

Dice and slice and hack (any old way) an avocado or two in a bowl. Then the same with about half as much tomato (fresh) as avocado you intend to use. Then juice and finely grate about 1 medium onion. Take a good trusty fork and whip (whip that is) all together. Salt and pepper and let it chill. Just before you serve, chop about a head of lettuce very small, add and whip into chilled stuff. Serve on leaf of lettuce, with ripe olives around it.

Foolproof and Fancy Free

This of course will turn out to be a tossed vegetable, but derned if the folks don't like it—it's not too troublesome and goes with most anything and anybody.

Tear up a head of lettuce in a bowl. (Big secret in all lettuce- and romaine-based salads is to *tear* the green stuff and *not* to cut it.) Now, start looking around for fresh vegetables. Cut up radishes, grate fresh carrots, slice some cucumbers, hack up some celery, use some finely sliced green onions, or the juice and pulp of an onion. Quarter some fresh tomatoes. Hey, before I forget —as you add each thing noted above, toss it around each time. Don't get excited and smash it and make it mushy, but use wooden implements and carefully toss. It helps and the juices stay in their proper places, not in the bottom of the bowl. Salt and pepper this good, then take any good mayonnaise and thin somewhat with cream, not too gooey. Let the bowl and ingredients chill, and the cup of thinned mayonnaise chill (separately). Mix again with dressing *just before serving*. (If you run across anything else around the kitchen you think would fit in with this, slap it in.)

Chive Dressing
(Oh brother, is this good!)

Let's break the monotony here and have a go at some dressings. Got some honeys, and honestly a couple I hate to give away, but to make you a grand slam saladier I suppose you'd better know the dressing type forthcoming.

Take a whole pint of thick (regular) mayonnaise and thin it with 3 tablespoons of wine vinegar. Right now add 2 teaspoons of finely chopped chives. Mess this up good and leave it stand quite a while so the gook and the chives permeate. It's okay to chill, and perhaps will be a shade better if you do. But make it at least a couple hours ahead of serving. *Tear* well-chilled lettuce in a bowl. Season with salt and *black* whole pepper. Splash in the chive dressing just as you are about to serve it. (Speaking of black whole pepper—and nobody was— use it in all salads that call for pepper. Huh? Makes a big difference.)

French Dressering (Oui)

Lots of folks like home-made French Dressing and here is a pretty quick and good example of same.

Mix a spoon or two of dry mustard with some paprika, black pepper, and salt. Add a squirt of Worcestershire and catsup and finally a smash of vinegar and salad oil. Whip. Ya got it. I'd like to say here that in all these salad dressings or any other cooking combination I can do better in blending by smelling instead of tasting. Try it. If it smells good, it tastes good.

Russian Dressing

What do you say some day when we feel fancy we whip up a batch of trick dressing. It's sort of a Russian deal worth a try.

First, for about 10 minutes, cook together 1 cup of

sugar and 1 cup of water. Then get a saucepan and slap in ¾ cup of tarragon vinegar, same amount of salad oil, 1 teaspoon of pepper, and a large tablespoon of salt. Now add a small onion and its juice. Smash it so you save the juice too. Best splash in about a tablespoon of Worcestershire and a whole cup of catsup. Smash up a half clove of garlic and then let this whole mess simmer at least 10 minutes. I don't know why but this always tastes and seems so different. Anyway as I have said— it's worth a try, and will surprise you, I'm sure.

Bailey's Bottled

Very fine to have on hand and the longer it stands the better, but it's good the first day you make it too.

To make a pint bottle do it this way. Take a small crock, and put in about ½ cup of olive oil. Add almost as much *cider* vinegar. Salt and pepper, garlic salt to taste (plenty), a dash of wine vinegar, the juice of a whole lemon, and several dashes of paprika. Needn't bother stirring too much now, but when you use it, stir it. Pour this in a pint bottle and keep in refrigerator. Each time you use it really shake it up. This will go on head or romaine lettuce. If you want to be cute and wilt a bit of leaf lettuce, then fry a few strips of bacon, let them be de-greased on some paper, but add a good healthy squirt of the bottled dressing to the bacon grease

Saludas to Salads (Si)

and wilt the leaf lettuce in that. Mighty fittin' and the folks will go for it.

De Luxe Dressing
(Fancy name I just thought of)

Here's a delicious dressing that defies people to figure out what-all is in it. A trick combination to be sure, but when the neighbors, kin, and family have at it and relish it, you'll purr with pride. The art of purring with pride should be used by all cooks.

Let's line up all the dry stuff first and mess around with it: 1 cup of sugar, a teaspoon of salt, only ¼ teaspoon of pepper, and chuck in ½ teaspoon of paprika. (Sneak this in, it's a fooler) 1 teaspoon of celery salt. Oh well, put in a teaspoon of mustard too. Now stir that around a little bit and get it good and mixed. Next, students, we take the wet stuff in another vessel. Yep, ¾ cup of tarragon vinegar, 1½ cups of salad oil. A half cup of catsup, 2 tablespoons of grated onion, and 1 clove of garlic minced and reminced. Now, if you've been paying attention you've mixed the dry stuff already. In the other bowl with the wet stuff mix 'er up good. You can keep these in readiness separate, and mix as needed, or put the whole batch in something (this all comes out at about ¾ of a quart) and shake it like thunder when you use it. I am sure it's better to mix things separately, as I have shown you above. I've tried it both ways and separately comes out best. Please, please don't ask me why, but by golly it works better. Then, I put it in a jug and forget it till I need it.

Joy Salad Dressing

Joy is the name of the girl that knew about this. She's a hair bender at the famous House of Westmore. Dorothy is her first name (no, I don't have my hair curled, haven't enough), but anyway do try this dressing. It's for romaine lettuce only.

Rub a salad bowl with a garlic button. Rub it good and hard and if a little smashes, leave it in the bowl. Now take a good-sized hunk of Roquefort cheese (about 2 inches by 4 inches) or to taste, and smash it up good with quite a bit of olive oil or salad oil. Add thick cream, either sweet or sour, and stir and whip until it is well mixed. I like it fairly thick, but that's up to you. This dressing gets better and better as you experiment with it as everyone likes their dressing a little different from others. Fiddle around with it, and this salad with red meat is perfect.

Bailey's Slickest

This, kiddies, is my favorite dressing. If you try this and do as directed you'll love me forever in the salad department. Fine stuff and keeps getting better the longer it stands. (Which reminds me, a Mrs. Schlictine was a big help with this one.)

Take a pint bottle of good oil mayonnaise and add ½ cup of good chili sauce (*not* catsup), 1 tablespoon of finely grated onion, and ¼ cup of cream (half and half). Smash up 2 medium size cloves of garlic. Smash 'em really smashed. Add a tablespoon of cider vinegar, 1 tablespoon sweet relish, and 2 tablespoons salad oil or olive oil. I stir this up by hand a little while, then put it in an electric mixer and mix it slowly for about 5 minutes till it's really blended. If you think of this in time, make it ahead so it can stand in the refrigerator overnight before using—ya don't have to, but it's better. I've used this slicker on a lot of things. If you're frying hamburgers, use a little on the sandwich with lettuce. Add a little Worcestershire and tabasco and use it to marinate steak before broiling or barbecuing.

Which reminds me. Saving is a very valuable asset, but in all recipes like the one above, or any recipe in fact, don't skimp on the ingredients you use. Get the very best you can, if it does cost a few cents more. And while I'm lecturing, be careful in all salads that if it says tarragon, use it—but if it says cider, use cider. I ruined a lot of dressings at first because I didn't think there was that much difference. I got caught . . . don't you.

A Flo and Zoe

Flo and Zoe are two gals I know. What they know, I'm going to show. It's a salad that's fine, good anytime—but the salad I know from Flo and Zoe, is a salad that'll go, and my heartfelt thanks to Flo and Zoe.

Two ladies' names, consequently better jot down two salads. They are similar, about alike, but maybe someone at the house will like one better than t'other. So here are both of them almost at once.

Take some lemon jello and make it like you always do *except* use warmed tomato juice instead of water. After you have mixed it good and before it hardens, add enough cottage cheese or Philadelphia cream cheese to make it pretty.

Next salad: Do the same thing as above, but instead of tomato juice use a can of vegetable soup. Same process. Now put 'er in the icebox (whichever method) and let it harden as per making regular jello. I've used regular ice trays for this so they harden in cubes.

Are you ready to serve? Okay. Make a nest of lettuce, and plank the jello mixture in the center. Around the edges in sections put sliced sweet pickles, cold cauliflower buds, and cold, very tiny canned peas. This is a beautiful thing to behold and a good salad to have and hold. Now cooks and chefs, let's see you go, and again my thanks to Flo and Zoe.

Can-Opener Cutie

Did you ever heave a sigh and pleasantly mumble to yourself, "Well, thank goodness that meal is cooked!" Then on the last rumble of the mumble discover that lo and behold you had forgotten to make a salad. That's happened to me several times, and if you are honest you'll admit the same omission. Now once in the grand town of Pittsburgh we were cordially entertained at one of our many friends'. She had gotten home a little late—the main course had been cooked and she was about ready to serve when it dawned on her—no salad. Thus the Can-Opener Cutie.

Take that sturdy instrument of love and open a can of kidney beans, and a can of small peas, mix 'em and add ½ cup of chopped celery. Boil thunder out of an egg and dice it, shred on canned pimento, season with salt and paprika, and just dash enough bottled French dressing to moisten this. Put this on some lettuce leaves, some mayonnaise on top, serve and cease worrying. Don't just save this for an emergency, use it often as it's good, healthful, quick. The only thing wrong could be the fact you can't find the can opener. In that crisis, I have this to say. Good luck.

Can-Opener Asparagus

Speaking of the can-opening implement, let us lend our talents to this usage.

Can-open a can of asparagus and drain. Then, put it in some French dressing to which you have added a little chopped pickle. Leave it be there a while, then when ready to serve take it out (do not drain), and over asparagus sprinkle a mixture of grated cheese and finely chopped hard-boiled eggs. Serve in a lettuce nest and I'm sure you will like. We like. Hope U like.

Roquefort Molds

Here's a way out of last minute dressing making. Make this the day before, 'cause there's other dressing to be done when guests arrive.

Soak $\frac{1}{2}$ tablespoon of gelatine in $\frac{1}{4}$ cup of cold water and dissolve over hot water. Now mash 3 packages of Roquefort cheese spread and mix with $\frac{1}{2}$ cup of milk. Mix with the dissolved gelatine and add $\frac{1}{4}$ chopped stuffed olives, ½ cup of finely chopped celery, and ½ teaspoon of lemon juice. Season with a bit of salt and pepper, then fold in 1 stiffly beaten egg white, and at the last add ½ cup of whipped cream. Place in individual molds in the refrigerator until firm. You can serve these molds on a big platter with French dressing in the center and alternate molds with something that makes it look keen. White asparagus tips, halved tomatoes, hunks of lettuce, or just anything like that. It can be made to look wonderful and believe me it is always a hit.

The cake has fallen!

CHAPTER THIRTEEN

DESSERTS

> *When you come to the end of a perfect meal*
> *And you're full and stuffed (so you feel)*
> *Come what may*
> *No matter what you say*
> *Kids—that dessert is on its way.*

It has come to pass that since the year One of cooking, desserts are a necessary finis to meals. Usually after one is so full his eyes are closing, the host or hostess will prance on with a dessert, floating with whipped cream, under which is hiding a seventeen-egg cake with a chocolate underpinning trussed up with ladyfingers au gratin. Now in this next brief chapter of desserts, I'm going to stick to simple and light things. If you go in for the heavy type dessert, that's your worry, not mine. I'm too fat as it is, and I don't think dessert helps that ailment. Now on this page I have the answer to every cook's prayer as to what to have for dessert. This I shall tell you, and then you thumb through the rest of this chapter at your own risk and leisure.

Bailey's Secret Dessert

I do want you to know my secret and special dessert and I trust it won't come as too much of a surprise. *You know what I do?*

I send someone to the corner drugstore and ask them to pick up a quart of ice cream. I always keep some cookies on hand so I'm all set. Now here's the two-way secret on that. I have my wife buy the cookies in advance, and the guy or gal I send to the drugstore uses his own money for the ice cream. Thus my net loss is not a net loss, but no loss at all. If they complain about the dessert (and they never have), tell them to call either the drugstore or the cookie company. Now there, folks, is one of my greatest secrets, all included in the price of the book.

Pearl's Punkin Pie

She's a friend of ours and I won't give you her whole name as it's in the book someplace else—but I will give you this great way to make pumpkin pie. We like pumpkin pie for two reasons—first it's usually good this way, and second you only have to make one crust for it. Well, here's to it, and happy desserting.

Desserts 175

Mix together one cup of pumpkin (smashed either live or canned), 1 tablespoon of flour, and ¾ cup of sugar. After good and mixed, add 1 beaten egg, a tablespoon of molasses, ¼ teaspoon of salt, ½ teaspoon of cinnamon, ½ teaspoon of ginger, ½ teaspoon of nutmeg. Then 1 tablespoon of melted butter and 1 cup of warm milk. Pour this into unbaked pie crust (already in a pie tin) and bake in a hot oven of at least 450° for about 10 minutes, then reduce heat to medium (350°) and cook for about an hour. For the pie crust use 1 cup of flour, ⅓ cup of shortening, and 3 tablespoons of ice water— or easier yet, a box of prepared piecrust mix. My only comment on the above is that you *can't* make a punk punkin pie this way. Never have yet, and neither will you.

Cutie Cup

Cutie Cup is named after an old friend of mine. It's a good thing she won't read and catch me in this book, because the word old would bother her, and thus she would bother me, and we shouldn't be bothered when writing a book that includes a Cutie Cup dessert. Never mind my old friend, but do mind how to make this wonderful and simple dessert. (Now please start this early as it is better the longer it is made—in fact, the day before you want it is swell.)

Take one package of raspberry jello and one package

of vanilla pudding, and make them separately in the usual way. Put them in the icebox to chill, let them thicken a bit, but *not* set, then put together in one bowl and whip the very dickens out of them till they are really blended. Now put in molds or dessert dishes and let harden. When you serve, either use a dash of thick cream or whip a little of same and top with a cherry. That's all there is to it and you'd be surprised at the oooohs and ahhhhhhs that come forth. Good luck to the Cutie that thought of the cup, and young old friend.

Peachy Peach Melba

This is so simple it's almost silly, yet it is mighty fine. The fact it has a little added zest and hardly any time to invest makes it a worthwhile dessert.

First, have on hand a bit of vanilla ice cream. Then take that "cooker's friend," the can opener, and de-lid a large can of peaches. Cut the peaches in small hunks and put in a pan with a couple of jiggers of cooking brandy. Cook with a low flame for about 5 minutes and then add some currant jelly, keep adding and stirring until thick. When thick (momentarily) serve this hot over both ice cream and white cake. Slick and tasty as the dickens, and looks like a million dollars. Forget the other involved Peach Melba gags that are so intricate and do it this way, saving time, money, and wear and tear on your dessert nerves. I made a grave error once and used a darkish cake under the ice cream. Don't ever make that same mistake. OOOOO was that awful. Marble, white, or angel food is the best. I know.

One Egg Loafing Cake

An Edna Parkinson (of the Ed Parkinsons of Great Falls, Montana) is a good but fairly lazy cook. She whips up this cake in nothing flat, and I've never seen the cake go flat—as is a thing that happens to so many cakes. This is a rather stingy way (but good) to make a dessert. We like it and so will you, I'm sure, and it's a loafing job to be sure.

Bust an egg (fresh egg, please) in a cup and fill it up with sweet milk (sweet, please). Beat this well and then add a cup of sugar and a smiggin' of salt, and then beat again. Now that's over, so you next sift 1½ cups of flour and 2 teaspoons of baking powder. Sift, did I say? Ya. Sift it 3 times (no fooling). Now after the third sifting add to the other ingredients and beat in 1 tablespoon of melted butter. Guess what you do next. You guessed it. Grease a pan or baking dish, pour batter in, and bake until done. For frosting just mash up some of those chocolate bits, add a bit of sugar and cream, boil and smear over the top of the cake. I always like white cake with chocolate frosting. If you have a special chocolate frosting, why don't you use it? Edna (being lazy) always uses the above.

Cake Lemon

Here now is a two- or three-layer cake with this wonderful lemon filling and icing. Naturally if you want three layers you had better have three cake-baking tins —if you've only got two tins make a two-layer cake. Outside of good old Lemon Pie, this is the best lemon dessert I know of, thus it got its name Cake Lemon. First the cake, then the filling, and then the icing.

Cake: 1 cup of sugar, ½ cup of butter well creamed. The yolks of 3 eggs (save whites for icing). 1 cup of milk and 1⅔ cups of all-purpose flour sifted with ¼ teaspoon of salt and 2 even teaspoons of baking powder. Now to this add the juice of 1 lemon. Stir until smooth and put in individual baking tins (according to the number of layers you have in mind).

Filling: 1 egg yolk beaten with ⅓ cup of sugar, the juice of another lemon, 2 teaspoons of flour, and add ⅔ cup of boiling water, a little salt. Now boil this until it thickens, cool, and spread between the cake layers (two or three) and on top layer too.

Icing: 2 egg whites unbeaten. 1½ teaspoons of light corn syrup, 5 tablespoons of cold water and a little salt. Beat together until light and place in double boiler, stirring constantly until it is thick enough to spread (5 or

Desserts

6 minutes). Remove from fire and add the juice of another lemon and stir same in. There you have it—and believe me, when you have it, you got a real swell dessert. Ah . . . Cake Lemon, I love you.

Mahogany Cake

Mahogany Cake. Hmmm. Isn't that a name for you? Marble, Burnt Sugar, Willow, Devil's Food, all kinds of names, but I had never heard of Mahogany (cake) until this Mrs. Wade (whose biography is elsewhere) made it. It's wonderful, but may sound a little involved, so don't be scared. I'll list the stuff first and explain how she does it—and I mean she really does it good.

Kindly assemble 1½ cups of cake flour that has been well sifted, 2 squares of bitter chocolate, ½ cup of boiling water, 1½ teaspoons of baking powder (level), ½ teaspoon of salt, 4 tablespoons of shortening, 1 cup of sugar, 2 eggs, and ½ cup of sour milk. Then 1 teaspoon of soda and 1 teaspoon of vanilla. All set? Keen. Now then, melt the chocolate over hot water, add ½ cup of boiling water, and stir until thick. Cool it. Put baking soda, salt, and flour together, and sift 3 or 4 times. Work shortening until creamy and add the beaten egg yolks, then flour mixture and sour milk alternately. Please put the soda in chocolate mixture and add stiffly beaten egg whites and vanilla. Mess 'er up good and bake in 2 layers (oven

350°) for 25 minutes. Ya don't have to bother with any icing or frosting, as this is good just the way it comes. Hope you like it as well as we did, and I'll bet you will.

Desserts to Dash Off

Many times halfway through a meal the host or hostess will suddenly realize there's nothing for dessert. If that should happen to you (as it does to all of us) please bear in mind these little gags that will suffice in emergencies.

1. Cube some fresh oranges, put them in fruit cups or long-stemmed glasses, and liberally sprinkle over the whole thing some shredded coconut.

2. Use all the fresh fruit you can find in the house like apples, pears, tangerines, and cheese. Jack cheese (no relation) is good, or any other kind of cheese on hand.

3. Take some Hershey bars (almond), break them up in small hunks, and serve them with cold, fresh milk.

4. Nuts.

5. Forget the whole thing and serve them coffee in the front room.

FINIS

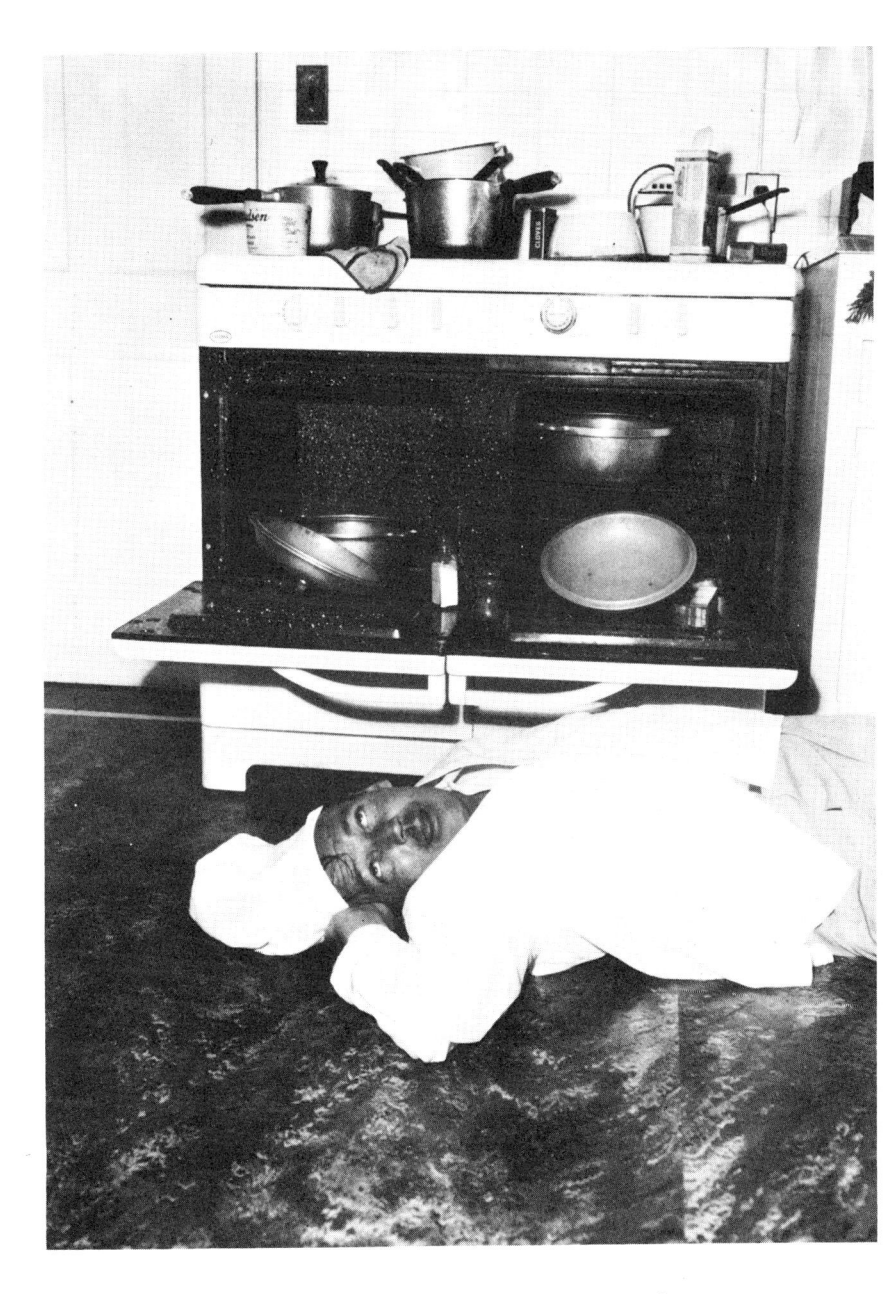

When you come to the end of a perfect meal....

INDEX

Ah gratin ah, 86
American-style guylas, 36
Appraised braised ribs, 43-44
Asparagus, can-opener, 170
Avocado
    smash, 161
    smash with bacon, 140

Bacon
    with avocado, 140
    with cheese, 140
    with sardines, 140
    with spinach and noodles, 134-35
Bacon avocado smash, 140
Bailey chips, 79
Bailey's bottled dressing, 164-65
Bailey's Iowa baked beans, 109-10
Bailey's secret dessert, 174
Bailey's slickest dressing, 167
Bailey's swiss steak, 119-20
Baked beans, Bailey's Iowa, 109-10
Baked potato spinochi, 81-82
Baking of beans á la Bailey, 110-11
Ball of the corned beef, 135
Ball of the potato, 76-77
Beans
    Bailey's Iowa baked, 109-10

Baking, á la Bailey, 110-11
    can-opener cutie, 169
    navy beans lambie, 29
    Spanish bean pot, 120-21
Beef
    beef hunk humdinger, 132
    chipped beef creamed, 33
    slumgullion, 33-34
    souféed beefola, 30
    stroganbailey, 25
Beets that beat beets, 155
Big baked veal cutlet, 37-38
Broccoli, marcelled, 68-69
Buckeroo potluck, 49-50
Burrage porrage, 65-66

Cabbage
    common, 152-53
    with sausage, 47-48
Cake
    lemon, 178-79
    mahogany, 179-80
    one egg loafing, 177-78
Canapés
    bacon avocado smash, 140
    celery stuffin', 143
    cheese-bacon-blitz, 140
    coleslawed ham slaw, 144
    creamed white and green, 145
    cucumber cutie, 142

liver in an egg, 142
miniature meat pies, 141
Roquefortish smear, 143-44
sardine-stuffed bacon, 140
sneak meat rolls, 141
sticks of cheese, 146
stuffed sliced square rolls, 144-45
Can-opener asparagus, 170
Can-opener cutie, 169
Casserole
  noodleburger, 45
  noodling, 130-31
  with tuna, 133-34
Cauliflower ear special, 154-55
Celery and stewed ham hunk, 132
Celery stuffin', 143
Cheese sticks, 146
Cheese-bacon-blitz, 140
Chicken
  in a port, 21-22
  Carolyn, 38-39
Chili
  con carne, homemade, 124-25
  potatoes, 86-87
Chinese
  chop suey home choice, 42-43
  egg foo yong, 102
  rice Chinatown, 151
  roast pork Chinatown, 30
Chipped beef creamed, 33
Chive dressing, 162-63
Chop suey home choice, 42-43
Chops of lamb en vino, 26
Chops of pork en loaf, 26-27
Chork pop pie, 46-47
Coffee cake
  dude ranch dandy, 70-71
Coleslawed ham slaw, 144

Corn, 148-49
  in stuffing, 67-68
  in the husk, 116
  with zucchini, 154
Corn meal phfft, 91-92
Corned beef, ball of the, 135
Corny stuffin', 67-68
Creamed white and green, 145
Cucumber cutie, 142
Curry for cooking capers, 35-36
Cutie cup, 175-76

De luxe dressing, 165-66
Deep South ribs, 66-67
Dentist's Dutch oven, 69-70
Desserts
  Bailey's secret dessert, 174
  cake lemon, 178-79
  cutie cup, 175-76
  icebox freeze, 122
  mahogany cake, 179-80
  one egg loafing cake, 177-78
  peachy peach melba, 176-77
  Pearl's punkin pie, 174-75
  suggestions for, 180
Dude ranch dandy, 70-71
Dunstedter's Dandy, 55-56
Dunstedterssspareribsandsauce, 57

Eggs
  aloof omelet, 101-2
  Chinese egg foo yong, 102-3
  double boiler omelet, 105
  egg bread crumb batch, 99
  egg noggin, 93-94
  eggs sickbed, 93
  ham and, 103
  oiled, 99-100

INDEX

omelet espaniole, 106
poached, 98-99
scrambled, 101
super egg supper, 107
three-in-one omelet, 97-98
tomato egg basket, 104-5
tropical, 103-4
with liver, 142
with mushrooms, 100

Fish, 53
Flo and Zoe, A, 168-69
Foolproof and fancy free salad, 161-62
French dressing, 163
French fried Bailey—onions, 152

Geller's goulash, 57-58
Goulash
American-style, 38
Geller's, 57-58
Hungarian, 38

Ham
"cops" ham, 61-62
that am, 32-33
with celery, 132
with coleslaw, 144
with eggs, 103
Hamburger sandwiches, 115
Homemade chili con carne, 124-25
Hors d'oeuvres (see CANAPÉS)
Hungarian goulash, 36

Icebox freeze, Mrs. B's, 122

Jack's juliennes, 83-84
Joy salad dressing, 166

Kartoffel klosse, 84-85

Lamb
chops en vino, 26
leg luscious, 27-28
navy beans lambie, 29
shades of lamb shanks, 24
Late returner's ragout, 129-30
Legless pork roast, 40-41
Leftovers
beef hunk humdinger, 132
curry for cooking capers, 35-36
scalloped stuffs, 117-18
Liver in an egg, 142
Liver, riced, 48-49
Loafer's meat loaf, 39

Macaroni gratoni, 34-35
Mahogany cake, 179-80
Meat
and potato cake, 136
Dentist's Dutch oven, 69-70
loaf, 39-40
pie, 123-24
Mickey fine vegetables, 153
Miniature meat pies, 141
Mushroom and the egg, 100

Navy beans lambie, 29
Noodleburger casserole, 45
Noodles
in casserole, 130-31
noodleburger, 45
with spinach and bacon, 134-35
Nutty potato croquettes, 85-86

Old-fashioned sweet slaw, 160
One egg loafing cake, 177-78
Onions, French fried Bailey, 152

Patty-cake potatoes, 79-81

Patty sausage grits en circle, 41-42
Peach and cottage cheese salad, 160
Peachy peach melba, 176-77
Pear and cheese salad, 159
Pearl's peachy puffy soufflé, 63-64
Pearl's punkin pie, 174-75
Pickled rolled steak, 64
Pippin' pot roast, 22-23
Plainish pot roast, 31-32
Poaching production, a, 98-99
Pork
  chops en loaf, 26-27
  legless roast, 40-41
  pie with chops, 46-47
  ribs, 66-67
  roast pork Chinatown, 30-31
  stuffed leg of, 23-24
Pot roast
  Dunstedter's dandy, 55-56
  plainish, 31-32
Potato balls supreme, 84-85
Potato
  ah gratin ah, 86
  Bailey chips, 79
  baked with spinach, 81-82
  ball of the, 76-77
  balls supreme, 84-85
  cake with meat, 136
  Jack's juliennes, 83-84
  Kartoffel klosse, 84-85
  nutty potato croquettes, 85-86
  patty-cake, 79-81
  puffers, 88
  real new potato zeal, 87-88
  salad piperoo, 113
  scaloopie, 78
  seven come eleven (creamed), 77-78
  sweet spudatoes, 81
  tinero, 75-76
  with chili, 86-87
Ragout, late returner's, 129-30
Rare Welsh rarebit, 137
Real new potato zeal, 87-88
Ribs
  and sauerkraut, 17
  appraised braised, 43-44
  Deep South, 66-67
  spare, with sauce, 57
Ribzzzzzzz, 62-63
Rice
  Chinatown, 151
  Spanish, 127-28
  with liver, 48-49
Roast
  Dunstedter's dandy, 55-56
  legless pork roast, 40
  pippin' pot roast, 32
  plainish pot roast, 31-32
  pork roast Chinatown, 30-31
Rolls, stuffed, sliced, 144-45
Roquefort molds, 170-71
Roquefortish smear, 143-44
Russian dressing, 163

Salad dressings
  Bailey's bottled, 164-65
  Bailey's slickest, 167
  chive, 162-163
  de luxe, 165-66
  French dressering, 163
  joy salad, 166
  Russian, 163
Salads
  A Flo and Zoe, 168-69

INDEX

avocado smash, 161
can-opener cutie, 169
foolproof and fancy free,
   161-62
old-fashioned sweet slaw, 160
peach and cottage cheese, 160
pear and cheese, 159
salad Philly, 66
Roquefort molds, 170-71
with potatoes, 113
Sardine-stuffed bacon, 140
Sausage cabbage head, 47-48
Sausage patty with grits, 41-42
Scalloped stuffs, 117-18
Schloterbeck special, 72-73
Scramble special, 101
Season shrimp creole, 60-61
Seven come eleven potatoes,
   77-78
Shades of lamb shanks, 24
Shrimp creole, 60-61
Slumgullion, 33-34
Smooth, slick, souffléed beefola,
   30
Sneak meat rolls, 141
Soufflé
   Pearl's peachy puffy soufflé,
   63-64
   smooth, slick, souffléed beefola,
   30
Spaghetti with meat sauce, 59-60
Spanish bean pot, 120-21
Spanish rice, 127-28

Spare ribs with sauce, 57
Spinach
   ahhhhhh, 50-51
   bacon noodle-doodle, 134-35
   baked with potatoes, 81-82
   —lettuce á la wilted, 156
   slicker, 94-95
Squab super chief, 65
Staples, 15-17
Steak
   Bailey's swiss, 119-20
   pickled rolled, 64
   Schloterbeck special, 72-73
   steako pineapplo, 28-29
   steako supremo, 112-13
Sticks of cheese, 146
Stuffed leg of pork, 23-24
Stuffed veal chops, 50-51
Sweet corn in the husk, 116
Sweet spudatoes, 81

Tropical eggs, 103-4
Tuna, tricky, 128-29
Tuna casserole-like, 133-34

Veal chops with stuffin', 50-51
Veal cutlet, baked, 37-38

Walnut maindisher, 92
Welsh rarebit, 137
Wienie bake, 131

Zucchini corn puddin', 154